On the cover:

The name **"raccoon"** originated from the Indian word *arakun*, which means "he scratches with his hands." During the 1700s, American colonists dropped the "a" in *arakun*, and the name became raccoon. Common raccoons are intelligent and curious animals. They sleep during the day and hunt for food at night. Each hand and foot of the raccoon has five fingers and toes. The nimble fingers of the raccoon help it to climb trees and to search for food.

California Treasures

A Reading/Language Arts Program

Program Authors

Diane August
Donald R. Bear
Janice A. Dole
Jana Echevarria
Douglas Fisher
David Francis
Vicki Gibson
Jan E. Hasbrouck
Scott G. Paris
Timothy Shanahan
Josefina V. Tinajero

 Macmillan/McGraw-Hill

Contributors

Time Magazine, The Writers' Express, Accelerated Reader

Students with print disabilities may be eligible to obtain an accessible, audio version of the pupil edition of this textbook. Please call Recording for the Blind & Dyslexic at 1-800-221-4792 for complete information.

B

The McGraw-Hill Companies

Mc Graw Hill Macmillan McGraw-Hill

Published by Macmillan/McGraw-Hill, of McGraw-Hill Education, a division of The McGraw-Hill Companies, Inc., Two Penn Plaza, New York, New York 10121.

Printed in the United States of America

ISBN: 978-0-02-199968-2/3, Bk. I
MHID: 0-02-199968-6/3, Bk. I

3 4 5 6 7 8 9 (079/055) 12 11 10 09

Welcome to
California *Treasures*

Imagine raising butterflies at the edge of a rain forest, learning about penguin chicks in Antarctica, or reading about a rooster that likes to cook. Your **Student Book** contains these and other award-winning fiction and nonfiction selections.

Treasures Meets California Standards

The instruction provided with each reading selection in your **Student Book** will ensure that you meet all the **California Reading/Language Arts Standards** for your grade. Throughout the book, special symbols (such as ✔) and codes (such as **R 1.1.2**) have been added to show where and how these standards are being met. They will help you know *what* you are learning and *why*.

What do these symbols mean?

CA = Tested Standards in California

✔ = Skill or Strategy that will appear on your test

R = Reading Standards

W = Writing Standards

LC = Language Conventions Standards

LAS = Listening and Speaking Standards

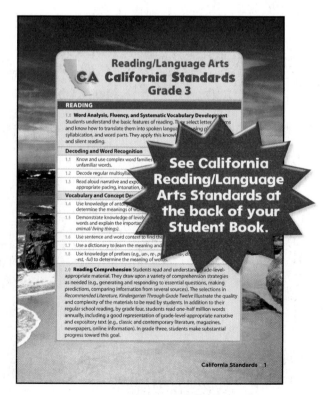

Reading/Language Arts
CA California Standards
Grade 3

READING

1.0 Word Analysis, Fluency, and Systematic Vocabulary Development Students understand the basic features of reading. They select letter patterns and know how to translate them into spoken language using phonics, syllabication, and word parts. They apply this knowledge to achieve fluent oral and silent reading.

Decoding and Word Recognition

1.1 Know and use complex word families unfamiliar words.

1.2 Decode regular multisyllabic words.

1.3 Read aloud narrative and expository text with appropriate pacing, intonation, and expression.

Vocabulary and Concept Development

1.4 Use knowledge of antonyms, synonyms, homophones, and homographs to determine the meanings of words.

1.5 Demonstrate knowledge of levels of specificity among grade-appropriate words and explain the importance of these relations (e.g., dog/mammal/animal/living things).

1.6 Use sentence and word context to find the meaning of unknown words.

1.7 Use a dictionary to learn the meaning and other features of unknown words.

1.8 Use knowledge of prefixes (e.g., un-, re-, pre-, bi-, mis-, dis-) and suffixes (e.g., -er, -est, -ful) to determine the meaning of words.

2.0 Reading Comprehension Students read and understand grade-level-appropriate material. They draw upon a variety of comprehension strategies as needed (e.g., generating and responding to essential questions, making predictions, comparing information from several sources). The selections in *Recommended Literature, Kindergarten Through Grade Twelve* illustrate the quality and complexity of the materials to be read by students. In addition to their regular school reading, by grade four, students read one-half million words annually, including a good representation of grade-level-appropriate narrative and expository text (e.g., classic and contemporary literature, magazines, newspapers, online information). In grade three, students make substantial progress toward this goal.

See California Reading/Language Arts Standards at the back of your Student Book.

California Standards 1

 Macmillan/McGraw-Hill

Unit 1

Personal Experiences
Let's Learn

THEME: Building Schools

THEME: Learning to Read

THEME: Those Special Books

CA STANDARDS PRACTICE: Show What You Know

Unit 2

History/Social Science
Neighborhoods and Communities

THE BIG QUESTION

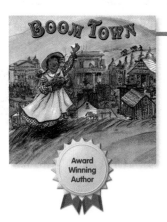

THEME: Birth of a Town

THEME: Starting a Local Business

Unit 3

Creative Expression

Express Yourself

Award Winning Selection

Award Winning Author and Illustrator

The **Big** Question

Why is learning important?

Theme Launcher Video

LOG ON Find out more about why learning is important at **www.macmillanmh.com**.

Whhat do schools, books, and museums have in common? They all help you learn. Learning helps you find out about the world around you.

In school you learn subjects, such as science and history. Outside of school you learn, too. You read street signs, recipes, and Web sites, and go to museums. Everywhere you go, you also learn how to make friends and get along with others.

Learning can help you become who you want to be. You may study science and become a doctor. You may study writing, and become an author. So keep learning about new things!

Research Activities

In this unit you will read about ways to learn and why learning is important. Choose something that you would like to learn more about. Research and write as much as you can about this topic. Write about what makes this topic interesting to you.

4

Keep Track of Ideas

As you read, look for ideas about learning. Some selections are about learning in school. Others are about learning at home or outdoors. Use the Layered Book. On the top section, write "Let's Learn." On each layer write connections from the weekly selections that tell about how the characters learn.

FOLDABLES®
Study Organizer

Unit Theme

Week 1
Week 2
Week 3
Week 4
Week 5

Research Toolkit

Conduct Your Unit 1 Research Online with:

Research Roadmap
Follow step-by-step guide to complete your research project.

Online Resources
- Topic Finder and other Research Tools
- Videos and Virtual Fieldtrips
- Photos and Drawings for Presentations
- Related Articles and Web Resources

California Web Site Links

LOG ON Go to www.macmillanmh.com for more information.

California People

Maria Azucena Vigil
Teacher
Ms. Vigil has been a California teacher for many years. She was the 1992 Teacher of the Year.

5

Teachers

Talk About It

You have teachers in school and outside of school. What kinds of things do you learn from them?

LOG ON ▶ Find out more about teachers at **www.macmillanmh.com**.

TINA'S TRYOUT DAY

by Amy Helfer

Tina woke up to her buzzing alarm clock. She rubbed her eyes and wondered why she was up so early. Then she remembered: it was tryout day!

THE BIG DAY

A few weeks ago, Tina decided she would try out for the Comets, her school's softball team. Tina ran downstairs to the kitchen. "Mom!" she shouted. "It's tryout day!"

"I know," answered Mom. "I made you breakfast."

"I'm too **nervous** to eat."

"You'll have more energy if you do," said Mom.

Tina still felt a bit sick, but she ate some breakfast anyway. Then she ran up to her room and **fumbled** into her clothes.

"Slow down!" Mom **chuckled**. "You'll use up all your energy before you get there."

ON THE FIELD

Tina got to the field and saw many girls already there. She suddenly felt unhappy.

"What am I doing?" Tina asked herself. "I'll never make the team."

Her mom gave her a hug. "That's **nonsense**," she said. "Get out there and do your best. You will be great!"

PLAY BALL!

The girls had to run, field, bat, catch, and throw balls. Even though Tina stumbled while fielding, she thought she did well.

Afterward, Tina was really tired and **trudged** off the field. One of the coaches called her name. "What do you think, Tina?" she asked. "Would you like to join the Comets?"

Tina forgot how tired she was and jumped high into the air. "Oh, boy!" she shouted. "Would I ever!"

Reread for **Comprehension**

Analyze Story Structure

Character, Setting, Plot Every story has characters, a setting, and a plot. They make up the story's structure. **Characters** are people in the story. The **setting** is when and where the story takes place. The **plot** tells all the events in the story. It has a beginning, middle, and end.

A Story Map helps you analyze the story structure. Reread the selection to find the characters, setting, and plot.

Character
Setting
Beginning
↓
Middle
↓
End

CA Comprehension

Genre

Realistic Fiction is an invented story that could have happened in real life.

Analyze Story Structure

Character, Setting, Plot

As you read, use your Story Map.

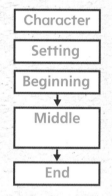

| Character |
| Setting |
| Beginning |
| ↓ |
| Middle |
| ↓ |
| End |

Read to Find Out

Why does Sarah try to avoid going to school?

10

FIRST DAY JITTERS

Award Winning Selection

by
JULIE DANNEBERG

illustrated by
JUDY LOVE

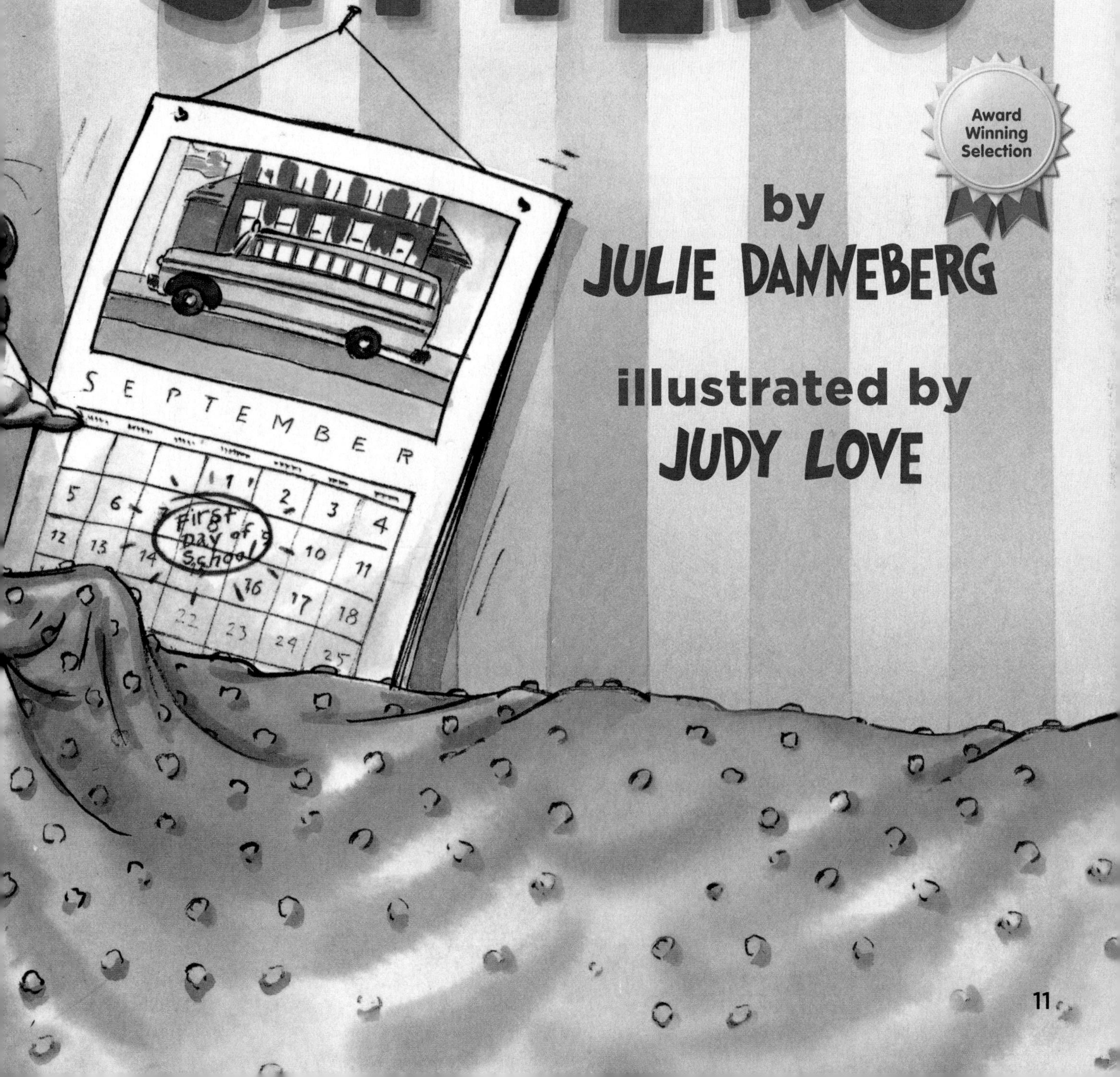

"Sarah, dear, time to get out of bed," Mr. Hartwell said, poking his head through the bedroom doorway. "You don't want to miss the first day at your new school do you?"

"I'm not going," said Sarah, and pulled the covers over her head.

"Of course you're going, honey," said Mr. Hartwell, as he walked over to the window and snapped up the shade.

"No, I'm not. I don't want to start over again. I hate my new school," Sarah said.

She tunneled down to the end of her bed.

Character, Setting, Plot
What plot events have taken place so far?

"How can you hate your new school, sweetheart?"
Mr. Hartwell **chuckled**. "You've never been there
before! Don't worry. You liked your other school, you'll
like this one. Besides, just think of all the new friends
you'll meet."

"That's just it. I don't know anybody, and it
will be hard, and ... I just hate it, that's all."

"What will everyone think if you aren't there? We told them you were coming!"

"They will think that I am lucky and they will wish that they were at home in bed like me."

Mr. Hartwell sighed. "Sarah Jane Hartwell, I'm not playing this silly game one second longer. I'll see you downstairs in five minutes."

Sarah
   tumbled
      out of bed.
         She stumbled into the bathroom.
         She **fumbled** into her clothes.

"My head hurts," she moaned as she **trudged** into the kitchen.

Mr. Hartwell handed Sarah a piece of toast and her lunchbox.

21

They walked to the car. Sarah's hands were cold and clammy.

They drove down the street.

She couldn't breathe.

And then they were there.

"I feel sick," said Sarah weakly.

"**Nonsense**," said Mr. Hartwell. "You'll love your new school once you get started. Oh, look. There's your principal, Mrs. Burton."

Sarah slumped down in her seat.

Character, Setting, Plot
How does Mr. Hartwell feel about Sarah's attitude?

"Oh, Sarah," Mrs. Burton gushed, peeking into the car. "There you are. Come on. I'll show you where to go."

She led Sarah into the building and walked quickly through the crowded hallways. "Don't worry. Everyone is **nervous** the first day," she said over her shoulder as Sarah rushed to keep up.

When they got to the classroom, most of the children were already in their seats.

The class looked up as Mrs. Burton cleared her throat.

"Class. Class. Attention, please," said Mrs. Burton.

When the class was quiet she led Sarah to the front of the room and said, "Class, I would like you to meet ...

... your new teacher, Mrs. Sarah Jane Hartwell."

OFF TO SCHOOL WITH
JULIE AND JUDY

AUTHOR

JULIE DANNEBERG knows all about teaching. She has been a teacher for many years and really enjoys it. Julie says that being around kids all day gives her lots of ideas for stories. She starts every day by working on her writing for an hour.

Another book by Julie Danneberg:
First Year Letters

ILLUSTRATOR

JUDY LOVE decided that she wanted to illustrate books when she was seven or eight years old. Judy gets ideas for her illustrations from her favorite hobbies: gardening, visiting museums, and making costumes for children's plays.

LOG ON ▶ Find out more about Julie Danneberg and Judy Love at **www.macmillanmh.com**.

CA **Author's Purpose**

Did Julie Danneberg write to inform or entertain readers in *First Day Jitters*? What details help you figure out the author's purpose?

 Critical Thinking

Retell the Story

Use your Story Map to help you retell *First Day Jitters.* Tell about what happened in the beginning, middle, and end of the story.

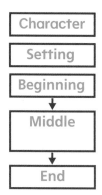

Character

Setting

Beginning

Middle

End

Think and Compare

1. Why was Sarah so **nervous** about going to school? Use details from the story's **plot** to support your answer. **Analyze Story Structure: Character, Setting, Plot**

2. At first, why might most readers think Sarah is a student? Use story details to support your answer. **Analyze**

3. How would you feel if you were a teacher on the first day at a new school? Explain. **Apply**

4. Why are many people nervous when they are in new situations? **Evaluate**

5. Read "Tina's Tryout Day" on pages 8–9. How is Tina's situation similar to Sarah's? How are Tina's and Sarah's reactions different? Use details from both selections in your answer. **Reading/Writing Across Texts**

How to Be a Good Citizen

by Jan Smith

A **citizen** is a person who lives in a **community**. Each citizen has certain rights and duties. Here is how you can be a good citizen.

Be Respectful Be kind and fair to everyone. Always tell the truth.

Be Responsible Follow the **laws**, or rules, of your **nation**, your state, and your town. Obeying the laws keeps you and the community safe.

Be Active Take part in school and community activities. Help your neighbors.

Be Informed Learn about your state and nation. Knowing your history can bring your community closer together.

Be Courageous Always try to help others, even when it is difficult. Dr. Martin Luther King, Jr., is an example of a good citizen. He fought for equal rights for all citizens. Follow these tips and you'll be on your way to becoming a great citizen!

Qualities of Good Citizens

Reading a Bar Graph

This bar graph shows the answers to a survey.
A survey asks what people think about something.

Survey Question:

What is the most important quality of a good citizen?

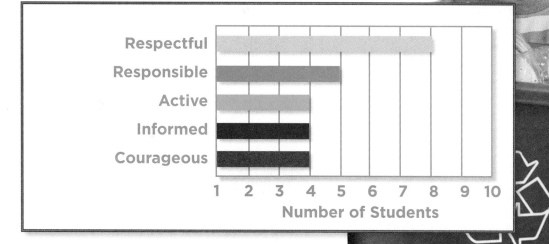

Respectful
Responsible
Active
Informed
Courageous

1 2 3 4 5 6 7 8 9 10
Number of Students

 Critical Thinking

1. Look at the bar graph. How many people answered the survey question? Which quality received the most votes? **Reading a Bar Graph**

2. What are some things you can do to be a good citizen? **Apply**

3. How is Sarah Jane Hartwell in *First Day Jitters* a good citizen? **Reading/Writing Across Texts**

 History/Social Science Activity

Work with a partner. Survey your classmates about what it takes to be a good citizen. Make a bar graph that shows your findings.

 Find out more at **www.macmillanmh.com**.

✔ **Focus on Moment**

When you **focus on moment**, your reader will see a strong image of what you are writing about.

Reading and Writing Connection

Read the passage below. Notice how author Julie Danneberg focuses on a moment of time.

An excerpt from
First Day Jitters

The author focuses on the moment when Mr. Hartwell first tries to get Sarah up. She uses details about what the two characters did and said to help us feel as though we're watching the moment.

"Sarah, dear, time to get out of bed," Mr. Hartwell said, poking his head through the bedroom door. "You don't want to miss the first day at your new school do you?"

"I'm not going," said Sarah, and pulled the covers over her head.

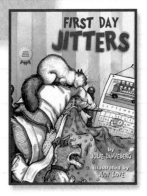

FIRST DAY
JITTERS

by
JULIE DANNEBERG
Illustrated by
JUDY LOVE

Read and Find

Read Kendall's writing below. What did she do to focus on a moment? Use the tips below to help you.

Fresh Baked Cookies!
by Kendall W.

I watched *my mom* carefully reach into the oven with the oven mitt. She slid out the tray of cookies. The heat from the cookies made the air above the cookie sheet shimmer. I closed *my eyes* and breathed in deeply to smell their *yummy* scent.

Read about the freshly baked cookies.

Writer's Checklist

✓ Does the writer pick a short amount of time and write a lot about it?

✓ Does the writer include specific details about her experience?

☑ Can you picture the **moment** the way Kendall experienced it?

THE POWER OF BOOKS

What are some ways in which we can enjoy the power of books?

 Find out more about the power of books at **www.macmillanmh.com**.

THE BIG SHOW

by Amelia Thomas

Sue and Jake watched the pouring rain make puddles in Sue's backyard. They tried to think of a way to keep busy indoors. Suddenly, Jake had an idea. "Let's do a play."

"That's a great idea!" said Sue. "We can write a play about a book we like."

Jake and Sue found a favorite **adventure** book about **exploring** a lost kingdom. It was an exciting story with a brave girl and her strong dog.

Sue and Jake wrote all afternoon. Then they phoned their friends Tomás, Nita, Jill, and Kate. "We are having **auditions** for our play," said Jake. "Come and read for a part."

The play sounded like fun, so all the friends came. Nita was chosen to play the explorer because she was a good actor. Of course, her dog Fred played the dog. The rest of the friends played the parts of the other adventurers.

Tomás and Jill made colorful posters covered with **sparkling** glitter to tell others about their wonderful show. Jake and Sue made a stage in Sue's backyard. Nita and Kate made costumes.

The next weekend, family and friends came to see the show. It was going well until the end. That's when Sue's cat leaped into the middle of the stage. Fred barked and chased the cat. Nita tripped over Fred. Sue started to cry. *The show is ruined*, she thought.

But then everyone stood up and clapped. "You were **fantastic**!" they yelled. "We want to see another show next week!"

Sue stopped crying and smiled. "We were a **success**! They liked us!" she said.

Reread for Comprehension

Make Inferences and Analyze

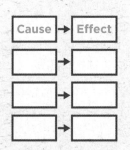

Cause and Effect

A **cause** is why something happens. The **effect** is what happens. Sometimes you need to analyze what happens in a story and make inferences about why these events happen. Reread the story. Use your Cause and Effect Chart to record causes and their effects.

Cause	→	Effect
	→	
	→	
	→	

Genre

Realistic Fiction is an invented story that could have happened in real life.

Make Inferences and Analyze

Cause and Effect
As you read, use your Cause and Effect Chart.

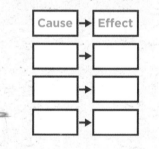

Cause	→	Effect
	→	
	→	
	→	

Read to Find Out

How do books help Grace achieve her dreams?

Amazing Grace

by Mary Hoffman
illustrated by Caroline Binch

Grace was a girl who loved stories.

She didn't mind if they were read to her or told to her or made up in her own head. She didn't care if they were in books or movies or out of Nana's long memory. Grace just loved stories.

After she had heard them, and sometimes while they were still going on, Grace would act them out. And she always gave herself the most exciting part.

Cause and Effect
What happens when Grace reads a book?

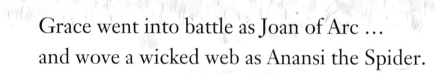

Grace went into battle as Joan of Arc …
and wove a wicked web as Anansi the Spider.

She hid inside the wooden horse at the gates of Troy....

She went **exploring** for lost kingdoms....

She sailed the seven seas with a peg leg and a parrot.

She was Hiawatha, sitting by the shining Big-Sea-Water … and Mowgli in the backyard jungle.

Most of all Grace loved to act out **adventure** stories and fairy tales. When there was no one else around, Grace played all the parts herself.

She set out to seek her fortune, with no companion but her trusty cat—and found a city with streets paved in gold.

Or she was Aladdin, rubbing his magic lamp to make the genie appear.

Sometimes she could get Ma and Nana to join in, when they weren't too busy.

Then she was Doctor Grace and their lives were in her hands.

One day Grace's teacher said they would do the play *Peter Pan*. Grace knew who she wanted to be.

When she raised her hand, Raj said, "You can't be Peter—that's a boy's name."

But Grace kept her hand up.

"You can't be Peter Pan," whispered Natalie. "He isn't black." But Grace kept her hand up.

"All right," said the teacher. "Lots of you want to be Peter Pan, so we'll have **auditions** next week to choose parts." She gave them words to learn.

When Grace got home, she seemed sad.

"What's the matter?" asked Ma.

"Raj said I can't be Peter Pan because I'm a girl."

"That just shows what Raj knows," said Ma. "A girl can be Peter Pan if she wants to."

Grace cheered up, then later she remembered something else. "Natalie says I can't be Peter Pan because I'm black," she said.

Ma looked angry. But before she could speak, Nana said, "It seems that Natalie is another one who don't know nothing. You can be anything you want, Grace, if you put your mind to it."

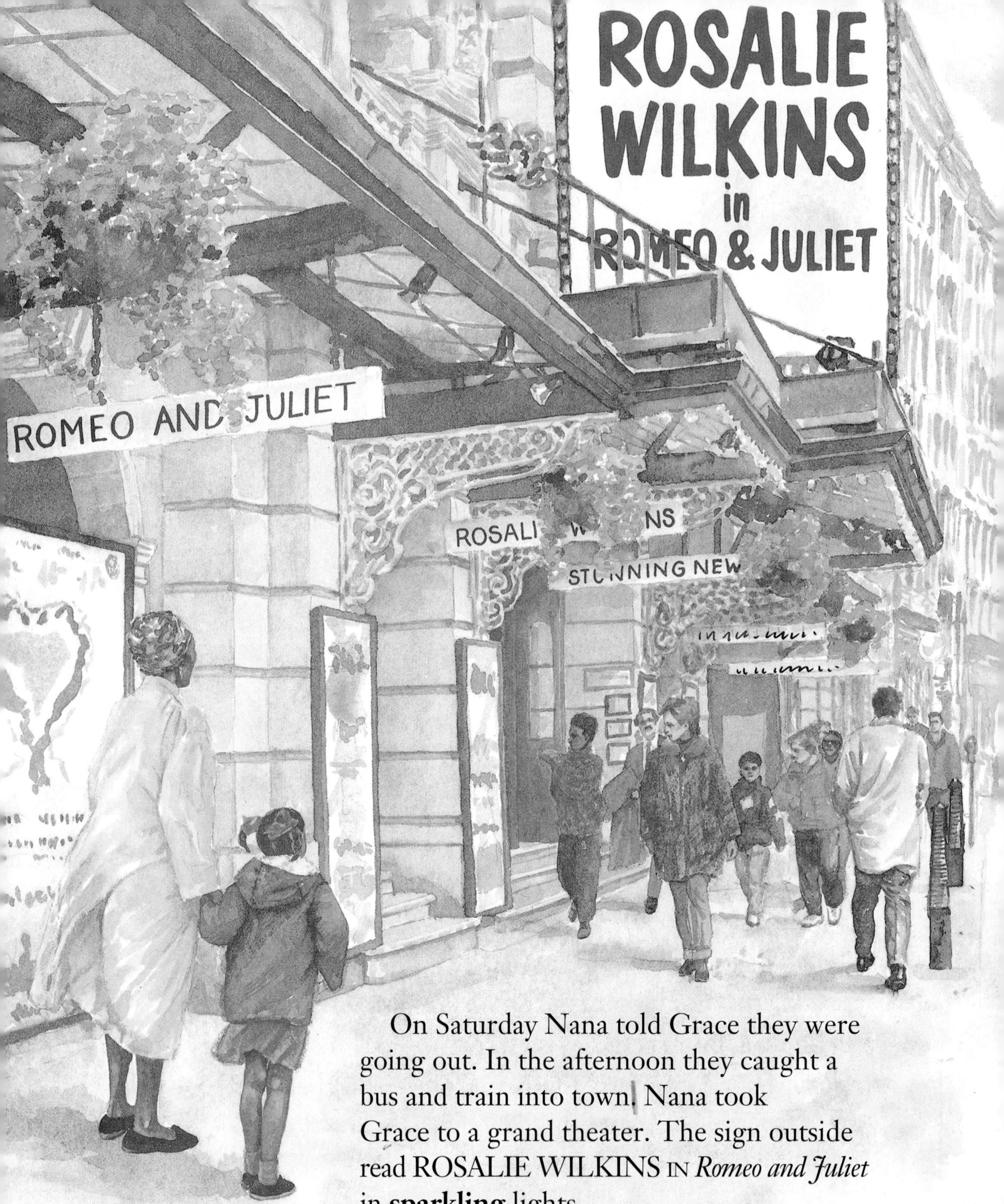

ROSALIE WILKINS in ROMEO & JULIET

ROMEO AND JULIET

ROSALIE WILKINS

STUNNING NEW

On Saturday Nana told Grace they were going out. In the afternoon they caught a bus and train into town. Nana took Grace to a grand theater. The sign outside read ROSALIE WILKINS IN *Romeo and Juliet* in **sparkling** lights.

"Are we going to the ballet, Nana?" asked Grace.

"We are, honey, but first I want you to look at this picture."

Grace looked up and saw a beautiful young ballerina in a tutu. Above the dancer it said STUNNING NEW JULIET.

"That one is little Rosalie from back home in
Trinidad," said Nana. "Her granny and me, we grew
up together on the island. She's always asking me do
I want tickets to see her Rosalie dance—so this time I
said yes."

After the ballet Grace played the part of Juliet, dancing around her room in her imaginary tutu. I can be anything I want, she thought.

On Monday the class met for auditions to choose who was best for each part.

When it was Grace's turn to be Peter, she knew exactly what to do and all the words to say—she had been Peter Pan all weekend. She took a deep breath and imagined herself flying.

When it was time to vote, the class chose Raj to be Captain Hook and Natalie to be Wendy. There was no doubt who would be Peter Pan. *Everyone* voted for Grace.

"You were **fantastic**!" whispered Natalie.

Cause and Effect
Why was Grace the best choice to play the part of Peter Pan?

The play was a big **success** and Grace was an amazing Peter Pan.

After it was all over, she said, "I feel as if I could fly all the way home!"

"You probably could," said Ma.

"Yes," said Nana. "If Grace puts her mind to it, she can do anything she wants."

Amazing Mary and Caroline!

Mary Hoffman was interested in stories at a young age. When she was in primary school, she wrote plays for her friends to perform. As an adult, she has written over eighty children's books. She has also written other stories about Grace, including Boundless Grace.

Another book by Mary Hoffman and Caroline Binch: *Boundless Grace*

Caroline Binch does more than draw pictures for children's books. She is a painter, a photographer, and a published author, too. She lives in England with her two dogs and cat.

LOG ON ▶ Find out more about Mary Hoffman and Caroline Binch at **www.macmillanmh.com**.

CA Author's Purpose

Fiction writers often tell stories that entertain or inform readers. What was Mary Hoffman's purpose for writing *Amazing Grace*? What clues in the story help you to understand the author's purpose?

 CA Critical Thinking

Retell the Story

Summarize the events in *Amazing Grace*. Then use your Cause and Effect Chart to help you understand why the events happened.

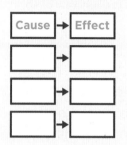

Cause	→	Effect
	→	
	→	
	→	

Think and Compare

1. What **causes** Grace to be upset when she comes home from school in the middle of the story? What was the **effect** on Nana? **Make Inferences and Analyze: Cause and Effect**

2. Reread pages 50–53 of *Amazing Grace*. Why do you think Grace's Nana took her to see the ballet? **Analyze**

3. Grace helped her class play become a **success**. What activity or show have you helped make successful? **Apply**

4. What do Grace and her classmates learn about themselves after the play? **Evaluate**

5. Read "The Big Show" on pages 36–37. Compare the play that the children made with the class play in *Amazing Grace*. How are they alike? How are they different? Use details from both stories in your answer. **Reading/Writing Across Texts**

Genre

Legends are stories that are handed down from the past and are based on the beliefs and traditions of a people or region.

✔ Literary Elements

Personification is when an animal or thing is given human characteristics in a poem or story.

THE STORYTELLING STONE

A Seneca story from the Northeastern United States by Joseph Bruchac

LONG AGO, there were no stories in the world. Life was not easy for the people, especially during the long winters when the wind blew hard and the snow piled high about the longhouse.

One winter day a boy went hunting. He was a good hunter and managed to shoot several partridge. As he made his way back home through the snow, he grew tired and rested near a great rock which was shaped almost like the head of a person. No sooner had he sat down than he heard a deep voice speak.

"I shall now tell a story," said the voice.

The boy jumped up and looked around. No one was to be seen.

"Who are you?" said the boy.

"I am Great Stone," said the rumbling voice which seemed to come from within the Earth. Then the boy realized it was the big standing rock which spoke. "I shall now tell a story."

"Then tell it," said the boy.

"First you must give me something," said the stone. So the boy took one of the partridge and placed it on the rock.

"Now tell your story, Grandfather," said the boy.

Then the great stone began to speak. It told a wonderful story of how the Earth was created. As the boy listened he did not feel the cold wind and the snow seemed to go away. When the stone had finished the boy stood up.

"Thank you, Grandfather," said the boy. "I shall go now and share this story with my family. I will come back tomorrow."

> The rock tells a story. This is an example of personification.

The boy hurried home to the longhouse. When he got there he told everyone something wonderful had happened. Everyone gathered around the fire and he told them the story he heard from the great stone. The story seemed to drive away the cold and the people were happy as they listened and they slept peacefully that night, dreaming good dreams. The next day, the boy went back again to the stone and gave it another bird which he had shot.

"I shall now tell a story," said the big stone and the boy listened.

It went on this way for a long time. Throughout the winter the boy came each day with a present of game. Then Great Stone told him a story of the old times. The boy heard the stories of talking animals and monsters, tales of what things were like when the Earth was new. They were good stories and they taught important lessons. The boy remembered each tale and retold it to the people who gathered at night around the fire to listen. One day, though, when the winter was ending and the spring about to come, the great stone did not speak when the boy placed his gift of wild game.

"Grandfather," said the boy, "Tell me a story."

Then the great stone spoke for the last time. "I have told you all of my stories," said Great Stone. "Now the stories are yours to keep for the people. You will pass these stories on to your children and other stories will be added to them as years pass. Where there are stories, there will be more stories. I have spoken. Naho."

Thus it was that stories came into this world. To this day, they are told by the people of the longhouse during the winter season to warm the people. Whenever a storyteller finishes a tale, the people always give thanks, just as the boy thanked the storytelling stone long ago.

CA Critical Thinking

1. How are Great Stone's actions like those of a real person's? Use details from the story in your answer. **Personification**

2. How do the stories help the boy and the people in the longhouse? **Analyze**

3. How are stories important to the people in the legend and Grace in *Amazing Grace*? Use details from the stories to support your answer. **Reading/Writing Across Texts.**

LOG ON ▶ Find out more about personification at www.macmillanmh.com.

Reading and Writing Connection

Writing

CA

✔ **Focus on Moment**

Good writers **slow down a moment** in time and describe the action using strong details.

Read the passage below. Notice how author Mary Hoffman focuses on a moment in time.

An excerpt from
Amazing Grace

The author focuses on the moment Grace learns an important lesson from her mother. We are able to picture this through the use of strong details.

Grace cheered up, then later she remembered something else. "Natalie says I can't be Peter Pan because I'm black," she said.

Ma looked angry. But before she could speak, Nana said, "It seems that Natalie is another one who don't know nothing. You can be anything you want, Grace, if you put your mind to it."

Read and Find

Read Brian's writing below. What did he do to focus on a moment? Use the tips below to help you.

A Special Day

by Brian J.

Read about a time I celebrated.

The candles were lit and my family started singing. My mind started to race as my mom walked over with the cake. What should I wish for? I puffed my cheeks and got ready to blow out my candles.

Writer's Checklist

☑ Does the writer write about one moment?

☑ Does the writer include specific details about that moment?

☐ Can you picture the **moment** the way Brian experienced it?

CA **Talk About It**

What do you think a school should look like? Are all schools alike?

LOG ON ▶ Find out more about building schools at **www.macmillanmh.com**.

Building Schools

Vocabulary

donate

unaware

members

contribute

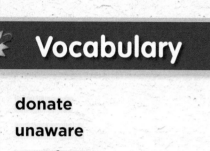

Juan Pierre plays for the Los Angeles Dodgers.

Play Ball!

Major League Baseball hit a home run in 2006 when it opened the Urban Youth Academy in Compton, California. The academy has four baseball fields, a huge clubhouse, and a learning center. There are baseball camps and after-school activities.

Kids ages 7 to 17 can take part for free at the academy. Do kids love it? Yes! Priscilla Mota, 10, plays softball and says that the academy has taught her many skills to improve her game.

Major League players **donate** their time to the academy. Director Darrell Miller, a former player for the Anaheim Angels of Los Angeles, tells future big leaguers that education is just as important as baseball. Education workshops teach kids how to do well both on and off the field.

Soon more kids will be able to have this learning experience. Major League Baseball is planning to build more academies in other cities. Kids in Miami; Washington, D.C.; and Pittsburgh may soon be hearing, "Play Ball!"

Students run drills on the field.

Top 5 Biggest Elementary Schools

The average United States elementary school has 400 to 600 students. Here are the elementary schools in the U.S. that have the most students.

Rank	School/Location	Number of students	
1	Miles Avenue Elementary, Huntington Park, California		2,709
2	Ernest R. Graham Elementary, Hialeah, Florida		2,449
3	Hoover Street Elementary, Los Angeles, California		2,372
4	Palm Springs North Elementary, Hialeah, Florida		2,245
5	Public School 19 Marion P. Jeantet, Corona, New York		2,164

Source: National Center for Education Statistics

👤 = 500 students

Freedom Fighter

In seventh grade, Craig Kielburger discovered that many children around the world were being forced to do hard and dangerous work. He knew that most people were **unaware** of the situation. So he began an organization called Free the Children.

Today, the children's charity has one million **members**. They have built more than 450 schools around the world and helped pay for medical programs in poor communities. People help in many ways. Some give money while others volunteer overseas. It's a great way to **contribute** to children's lives around the world.

Craig Kielburger and friends at a new school in Ecuador

LOG ON ▶ Find out more about types of schools at www.macmillanmh.com.

69

EARTH Smart

How do green schools help the environment?

Goodwillie Environmental School is friendly to the environment. Goodwillie is a green school in Ada, Michigan. Green schools do many things to help the Earth.

Green schools use less energy than regular schools. At Goodwillie, solar panels use the sun's power. The solar power heats the school in winter. This helps keep energy bills low.

The school also believes in using recycled items. Its walls and floors are made with recycled material. Even the outdoor deck is made from sawdust and recycled milk jugs!

Clara Cullen (left) and Seana Florida find frogs in Goodwillie's pond.

Students at green schools learn a lot about nature and the environment. The teachers and students at Goodwillie spend part of nearly every day outside, even in the freezing winter. Kids might collect sap from a tree, visit the school pond, or pick up trash along the road.

Kids tackle large projects, too. Some classmates work together to build a canoe. Others create a butterfly garden. Students also **donate** money or time to environmental groups.

Going to the Birds

The students at Goodwillie school also raise chickens. This farming lesson teaches kids about nature, the environment, and business. The chickens make eggs that are sold in the school store, which students run.

Molly Gaudette and Stephen Dozeman observe a tree's bark.

71

Everyone at Goodwillie pitches in to take care of the chickens. They **contribute** by feeding the chickens and taking turns cleaning the chicken coop. Manure that is cleaned from the coop is recycled. It makes compost for the school garden. Compost helps plants grow. Students at Goodwillie then study the plant growth in the garden.

Spencer Chan and Eleanor Schichtel feed the chickens.

Great Green Schools

Schools across the country are going green! In the next few years, Southern California alone plans to open 150 green schools. Why? Green schools are better for the environment and the people inside the schools. Students learn better in rooms that have natural sunlight. Green schools also have lower energy bills.

In Lick-Wilmerding High School in San Francisco, California, students create objects from natural and recycled materials. The cafeteria serves only healthful food. Most students ride energy-saving buses and trains to school instead of riding in cars. The school gets an A in helping the environment!

The Great Outdoors

As part of their studies, students at Goodwillie also study the life cycles of plants and animals. Instead of classrooms, they sometimes study in the woods and fields. "We write about some of the things we're seeing, such as the change in seasons," says Clara Cullen, 10.

Some **members** of a third-grade class are working on a project that will last about two years. They are studying the weather cycle. The students are figuring out how the weather helps or harms plants. Clara was **unaware** of what she could learn outside. Spending time in nature has opened her eyes. "It's amazing how much is out there," she says.

CA Critical Thinking

1. What does the writer mean by saying Goodwillie is friendly to the environment?

2. In what ways is your school green? In what ways is it not?

3. What could you do to make your school more green?

4. What are the **main ideas** in "Play Ball!" and "Earth Smart"? What opinion about these two different types of schools do both writers share?

Anna Veltman (left) and Rachel Wallace enjoy class outdoors.

Summer Break?

Do you have school in summer? Students in Oxnard, California, do. That's because schools in Oxnard are year-round schools. There are 1,483 year-round schools in California. In the United States, about 2 million students attend year-round schools.

All students in the United States have to go to school for 180 days each year. In regular school, kids go to class for about ten months and get two months off in the summer. Year-round schools break up the 180 days differently. Students usually get short breaks scattered throughout the year.

What are the benefits of year-round school? Experts say that students remember more when breaks are shorter. With less vacation time, teachers spend less time on review. That can add up to better grades. As a result, some schools say year-round students score higher on tests.

Still, not everyone is happy. Some parents say year-round school cuts into vacation time. Students say they miss out on summer activities, such as camp. Change could take some getting used to, but it's clear to see that there are many different ways to get your 180 school days.

Go on ▶

Directions: Now answer Numbers 1–5. Base your answers on the article "Summer Break?"

1. **Why do students in Oxnard, California, have school in the summer?**

   A   The schools in Oxnard close during the winter.
   B   The schools in Oxnard are year-round schools.
   C   The schools in Oxnard are open more than 180 days a year.
   D   The schools in Oxnard have too many students.

Tip
Look for key words.

2. **What do experts say about shorter breaks in the school year?**

   A   Students remember less.
   B   Teachers spend more time on review.
   C   Students remember more.
   D   Students may score lower on tests.

3. **Why are some parents not happy about year-round school?**

   A   They say they will never get used to it.
   B   They think it doesn't help their children's grades.
   C   They think it costs too much money.
   D   They say it cuts into vacation time.

4. **Do you think year-round schools are a good idea? Why or why not? Use details from the article to support your answer.**

5. **Compare and contrast regular schools with year-round schools. How are they alike? How are they different? Use details from the article in your answer.**

✏️ Write on Demand

CA

People often enjoy games and rides.

Think about a time you enjoyed a game or ride.

Now <u>write a story about</u> the time you enjoyed a game or ride.

Narrative writing tells a story about a personal or fictional experience.

To figure out if a writing prompt asks for narrative writing, look for clue words, such as <u>write a story about</u> or <u>tell what happened</u>.

Below see how one student begins a response to the prompt above.

The story events are told in a sequence that makes sense.

I gave my blue ticket to the man and ran to the horse I had chosen. I climbed up and held the gold pole with both hands. Loud music started, and the carousel began to turn.

My beautiful horse galloped up and down. Its saddle was painted bright red and yellow. The horse was grayish with smoky black spots. It was the best horse on the carousel!

When the ride stopped, I looked at the other people. Everyone was smiling. I guess they all enjoyed the ride, too.

Writing Prompt

Respond in writing to the prompt below. Write for 5 minutes. Write as much as you can, as well as you can. Review the hints before and after you write.

CA Most students like to play in the playground or park. Think of a time when you played in the playground or park. Now write a story about a time you played in the playground or park.

Writing Hints for Prompts

☑ Read the prompt carefully.
☑ Plan your writing by organizing your ideas.
☑ Support your ideas by telling more about each event.
☑ Use a variety of sentence structures.
☑ Choose words that help others understand what you mean.
☑ Review and edit your writing.

How can stories teach you about animals? How can stories teach you about the world around you?

 Find out more about learning to read at www.macmillanmh.com.

Learning to Read

THE BOY WHO CRIED WOLF

retold by Carole Bartell

There was once a young shepherd who lived in a village. This boy loved looking after his sheep. He did his job with **passion**. The villagers always told him what a good job he was doing. His work was easy to **admire**.

HAVING SOME FUN

One day the boy was bored. His mind wandered. He couldn't **concentrate** on watching the sheep. Then he thought of something wonderful to do. He thought it was a **splendid** idea.

He yelled, "Help! Wolf! A wolf is chasing the sheep!"

The villagers came running.

"Where is it?" one man asked.

"There's no wolf," the boy laughed. "I was just having fun."

"We are all busy working. You shouldn't be **bothering** us when there's no wolf!" he said.

Far away, a wolf looked at his watch and waited. He chuckled at his plot to fool the boy and the villagers.

THE NEXT DAY

The next day the boy was bored again. "Wolf!" he cried.

Once again the villagers ran up the hill but saw no wolf.

"Wolves are dangerous! They can harm you and the sheep!" they shouted angrily.

ONE DAY LATER

The next day the boy saw the wolf. He cried out, "Wolf! Wolf!"

"Time to run," said the wolf as he chased the sheep.

The villagers didn't come. When they saw the boy next, he was crying. His throat **ached** from crying for help.

"Why didn't you come when I called?" he asked. "A wolf chased all the sheep away."

"No one believes a liar, even if he is telling the truth," they said.

Reread for **Comprehension**

Generate Questions

Compare and Contrast Generating, or asking, questions as you read can help you compare and contrast characters, things, and events. To compare and contrast characters, tell how characters are **alike** and **different**. Reread the selection. As you read, look for character actions, traits, and feelings that you can **compare**. Use your Compare and Contrast Chart to help you determine how characters are alike and different.

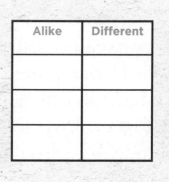

Alike	Different

Genre

A **Fantasy** is a story with characters, settings, or other elements that could not exist in real life.

Generate Questions

✓ **Compare and Contrast**

As you read, use your Compare and Contrast Chart.

Alike	Different

Read to Find Out

Why does the wolf go to school?

WOLF!

by Becky Bloom
illustrated by Pascal Biet

After walking for many days, a wolf wandered into a quiet little town. He was tired and hungry, his feet **ached**, and he had only a little money that he kept for emergencies.

Then he remembered. There's a farm outside this village, he thought. I'll find some food there . . . .

Compare and Contrast
How is the wolf like a real wolf? How is he different?

As he peered over the farm fence, he saw a pig, a duck, and a cow reading in the sun.

The wolf had never seen animals read before. "I'm so hungry that my eyes are playing tricks on me," he said to himself. But he really was very hungry and didn't stop to think about it for long.

The wolf stood up tall, took a deep breath …
and leaped at the animals with a howl—

"AaaOOOOOooo!"

Chickens and rabbits ran for their lives, but the duck,
the pig, and the cow didn't budge.

"What is that awful noise?" complained the cow. "I
can't **concentrate** on my book."

"Just ignore it," said the duck.

The wolf did not like to be ignored.

"What's wrong with you?" growled the wolf. "Can't you see I'm a big and dangerous wolf?"

"I'm sure you are," replied the pig. "But couldn't you be big and dangerous somewhere else? We're trying to read. This is a farm for educated animals. Now be a good wolf and go away," said the pig, giving him a push.

The wolf had never been treated like this before.

"Educated animals … educated animals!" the wolf repeated to himself. "This is something new. Well then! I'll learn how to read too." And off he went to school.

The children found it strange to have a wolf in their class, but since he didn't try to eat anyone, they soon got used to him. The wolf was serious and hardworking, and after much effort he learned to read and write. Soon he became the best in the class.

Compare and Contrast
Compare the wolf with the other students in the class. How is he the same? How is he different?

Feeling quite satisfied, the wolf went back to the farm and jumped over the fence. I'll show them, he thought.

He opened his book and began to read:

"Run, wolf! Run!

See wolf run."

"You've got a long way to go," said the duck, without even **bothering** to look up. And the pig, the duck, and the cow went on reading their own books, not the least impressed.

The wolf jumped back over the fence and ran straight to the public library. He studied long and hard, reading lots of dusty old books, and he practiced and practiced until he could read without stopping.

"They'll be impressed with my reading now," he said to himself.

The wolf walked up to the farm gate and knocked. He opened *The Three Little Pigs* and began to read:

"Onceuponatimetherewerethreelittlepigsonedaytheir mothercalledthemandtoldthem—"

"Stop that racket," interrupted the duck.

"You have improved," remarked the pig, "but you still need to work on your style."

The wolf tucked his tail between his legs and slunk away.

But the wolf wasn't about to give up. He counted the little money he had left, went to the bookshop, and bought a **splendid** new storybook. His first very own book!

He was going to read it day and night, every letter and every line. He would read so well that the farm animals would **admire** him.

Ding-dong, rang the wolf at the farm gate.

He lay down on the grass, made himself comfortable, took out his new book, and began to read.

He read with confidence and **passion**, and the pig, the cow, and the duck all listened and said not one word.

Each time he finished a story, the pig, the duck, and the cow asked if he would please read them another.

So the wolf read on, story after story.

One minute he was Little Red Riding Hood,

the next a genie emerging from a lamp,

and then a swashbuckling pirate.

"This is so much fun!" said the duck.

"He's a master," said the pig.

"Why don't you join us on our picnic today?" offered the cow.

And so they all had a picnic—the pig, the duck, the cow, and the wolf. They lay in the tall grass and told stories all the afternoon long.

"We should all become storytellers," said the cow suddenly.

"We could travel around the world," added the duck.

"We can start tomorrow morning," said the pig.

The wolf stretched in the grass. He was happy to have such wonderful friends.

Read Along with Becky and Pascal

Author
Becky Bloom was born in Greece but has traveled to many countries to work and go to school. She studied architecture at the University of California at Berkeley and now lives in the south of France with her husband and children. She has many different animals around her home, but no wolf.

Other books by Becky Bloom and Pascal Biet: *Leo and Lester* and *Mice Make Trouble*

Illustrator
Pascal Biet has lived in France his whole life. He was born in Saint-Laurent, in the north of France. He studied visual communication and design in Blois, France, and now he lives in Paris.

LOG ON ▶ Find out more about Becky Bloom and Pascal Biet at **www.macmillanmh.com**.

CA Author's Purpose

Wolf! mixes fantasy with reality. Did Becky Bloom want to inform or entertain her readers? What clues help you to understand her purpose?

Critical Thinking

Retell the Story

Retell the events in *Wolf!* Then use your Compare and Contrast Chart to help you compare and contrast the characters and events.

Alike	Different

Think and Compare

1. **Compare and contrast** the wolf with the pig in the beginning of the story. How are they alike and different? Use story details. **Generate Questions: Compare and Contrast**

2. Explain the steps the wolf takes to make friends with the cow, pig, and duck. Use story details in your answer. **Synthesize**

3. The animals in the story have a **passion** for reading and learning. Tell about a passion you have. **Apply**

4. Why did the animals like the wolf after he learned to read well? Explain your answer. **Analyze**

5. Read "The Boy Who Cried Wolf" on pages 80–81. Compare it with *Wolf!* In which story do the animal characters act more like real people? Use details from both selections in your answer. **Reading/Writing Across Texts**

The Truth About WOLVES

by Paul Netcher

For years wolves have been feared and misunderstood. They are the villains in many folk tales. How did these furry animals get such a bad **reputation**? It's because people think they're sneaky and always hunting for food.

The wolf's bad reputation is not truly deserved. It's time to set the record straight. Here is the truth about *Canis lupus*—the gray wolf.

Life in a Pack

Wolves do not like to live near humans. They prefer the company of other wolves. They live in groups called packs. A pack is made up of two parents and their newest **offspring**, or young. Sometimes other wolves become part of a pack, too.

Most packs have six to eight wolves. Some packs can have as many as 30 members!

Wolves often help each other. They live, hunt, and raise pups together. In fact, members of a pack always work together to hunt deer or moose.

Follow the Leader

Using Text Features

These text features help you make sense of what you read.

heading

boldface type

pronunciation

The wolves in a pack have a **hierarchy** (HIGH•uh•rahr•kee), or order. The pack leaders are called the *alpha* male and female. Each of the other wolves has a role, or job, within the pack.

italics

Raising the Pups

Pups are born in a well-hidden cave or dirt hole called a **den**. At first, the mother stays with the pups. She lets other members of the pack bring her food. After a few weeks, the mother goes off with the rest of the pack to hunt. Another adult may "baby-sit" the pups while she is gone. When the pack returns, they chew and spit up meat for the pups.

Young wolves learn how to hunt by playing. They also learn by watching other pack members.

Talking Like a Wolf

Wolves **communicate**, or give information to each other in different ways. Sometimes they use body movements to let other wolves know how they feel. Different howls also have different meanings. One howl calls the pack together. Another howl warns other packs to stay away. Even though many pictures show wolves howling during a full moon, wolves never howl at the moon! They are just communicating with the pack.

CA Critical Thinking

1. How can the heading and the word in boldface type on page 107 help you find information quickly? **Using Text Features**

2. What is your opinion of wolves after reading this article? Use details from the article in your answer. **Evaluate**

3. Use information in this article to tell how the main character in *Wolf!* is different from a real wolf. **Reading/Writing Across Texts**

Science Activity

Do more research about wolves. On the computer, write an article for younger students that tells what you learned. Use text features such as *italics, headings,* and *bold* or *colored type* to highlight important parts of your article.

LOG ON ▶ Find out more about wolves at www.macmillanmh.com.

Reading and Writing Connection

Writing

✓ Focus on Moment

Good writers **slow down a moment** in time by describing character details.

Read the passage below. Notice how author Becky Bloom focuses on a moment in her story.

An excerpt from *Wolf!*

The author focuses on the moment when the wolf finally gets the other animals to pay attention to his reading. By using focus, the author can include details about what each character does as the wolf starts reading.

Ding-dong, rang the wolf at the farm gate.

He lay down on the grass, made himself comfortable, took out his new book, and began to read.

He read with confidence and passion, and the pig, the cow, and the duck all listened and said not one word.

WOLF!
by Becky Bloom
illustrated by Pascal Biet

Read and Find

Read Robert's writing below. What did he do to focus on a character and an object? Use the tips below to help you.

My Best Catch Ever
by Robert R.

Crack! I heard the batter smash the ball with her bat. The ball flew up into the air, soaring higher and higher. I lost sight of it for a second when it passed the sun, but then I saw it coming right toward me! I locked my eyes on the ball and lifted my glove over my head. Thump! It dropped right in!

Read about when I caught the ball.

Writer's Checklist

✓ Does the writer pick one **moment** and write a lot about it?

✓ Does the writer use specific details about what happened in the moment?

☑ Do you get a clear picture in your mind of how Robert experienced this moment?

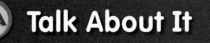

Talk About It

What books are special to you? How are they special?

LOG ON ▶ Find out more about special books at **www.macmillanmh.com**.

Those Special Books

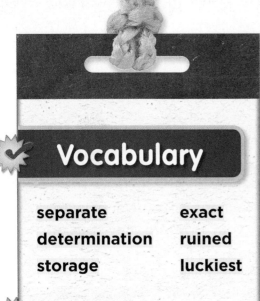

Pond Street Clubhouse

by Sylvia Medrano

On Saturday I went to the lumberyard with Dad to order lumber for the new garage. I saw the wood and got an idea.

"Hey, Dad," I said. "Could we build a clubhouse?"

"Probably not," said Dad. "I'll be too busy with the garage."

"But, Dad," I said, "you had a clubhouse when you were young."

Dad smiled and said, "I know, but first we have to build the garage."

I had to think of a way to get Dad to agree. "We can **separate** the clubhouse into two rooms," I said with **determination**. "The bigger one can be used as a **storage** room."

114

Dad thought about it for a moment. Then he said, "Let's wait to see if there is enough extra wood."

The garage supplies came the following weekend. There were huge piles of wood and a big box. It was a crate of nails and shingles for the roof. It looked like more than enough. When the truck left, Dad said, "Good news! We'll be able to build your clubhouse with the leftover wood when the garage is finished."

After a few weeks, it was time to start. A bunch of neighborhood kids came to help.

Dad let us measure the wood. Measuring has to be **exact** or else the pieces won't fit together. If Dad cut the wood too long or too short, our plans could be **ruined**. I knew we couldn't buy any extra wood.

When the clubhouse was finally finished, I was so thrilled. I made a sign and nailed it on the door. It said, "Pond Street Clubhouse—Welcome!" Now I have a great place to play. Am I the **luckiest** kid in town, or what?

Reread for **Comprehension**

Monitor Comprehension

Make and Confirm Predictions You can monitor your comprehension of a story by **making predictions** about what characters might do or what events might happen. Reread the selection. Use your Predictions Chart to keep track of your predictions about characters and events. Then check to see if your predictions were correct by writing **what happens**.

What I Predict	What Happens

Genre

Realistic Fiction is an invented story that could have happened in real life.

Monitor Comprehension

Make and Confirm Predictions

As you read, use your Predictions Chart

What I Predict	What Happens

Read to Find Out

How does the girl get her own room?

116

My Very Own Room

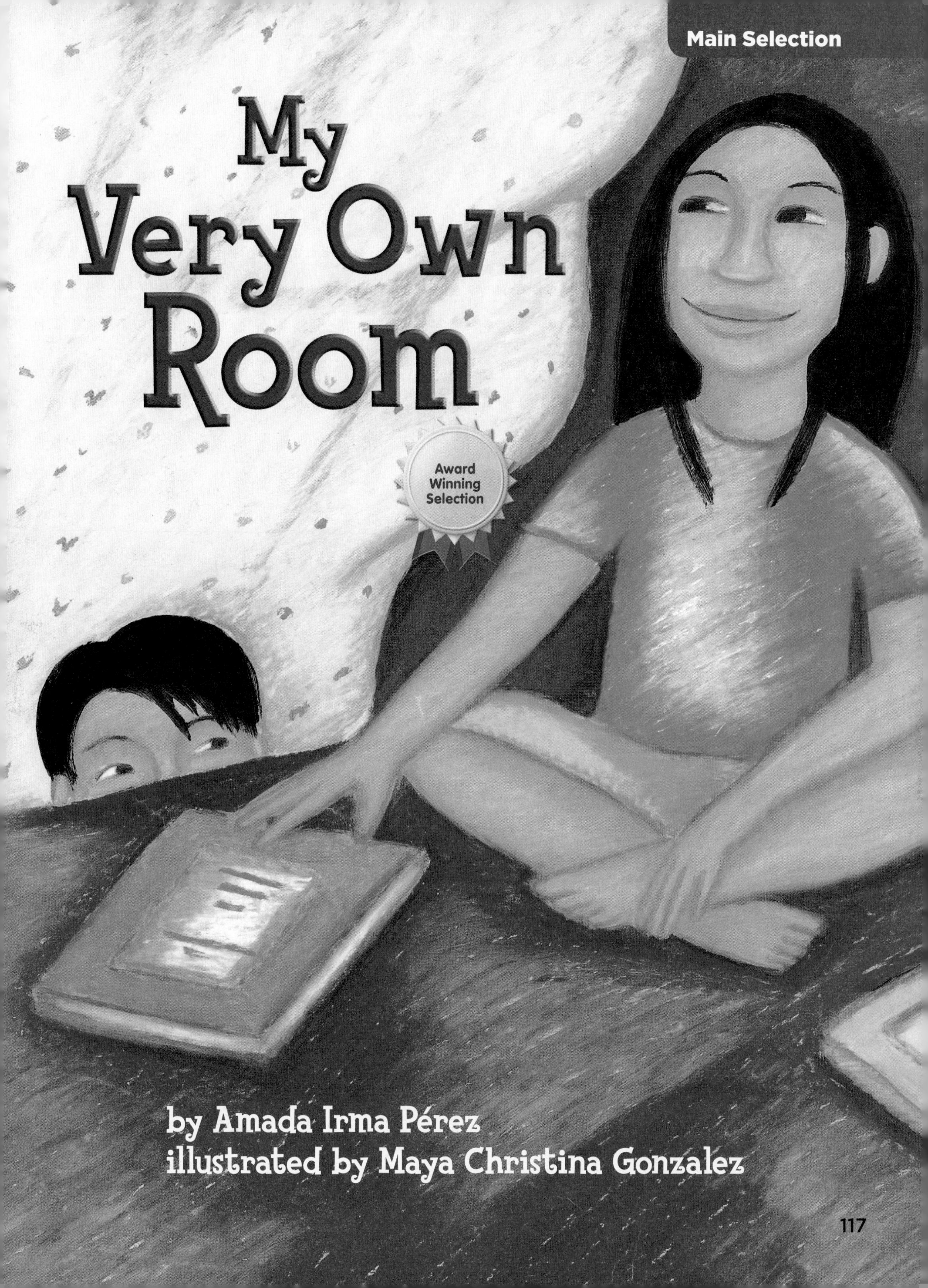

by Amada Irma Pérez
illustrated by Maya Christina Gonzalez

I woke up one morning on a crowded bed in a crowded room. Víctor's elbow was jabbing me in the ribs. Mario had climbed out of his crib and crawled in with us. Now his leg lay across my face and I could hardly breathe. In the bed next to ours my three other brothers were sleeping.

I was getting too big for this. I was almost nine years old, and I was tired of sharing a room with my five little brothers. More than anything in the whole world I wanted a room of my own.

A little space was all I wanted, but there wasn't much of it. Our tiny house was shared by eight of us, and sometimes more when our friends and relatives came from Mexico and stayed with us until they found jobs and places to live.

Once a family with eight kids (mostly boys!) lived with us for two months. It was noisy and a lot of fun. There was always a long line to use the bathroom, but the toilet seat was always warm.

Sometimes very early in the morning while everyone was still sleeping, I would climb up the crooked ladder that leaned against the elm tree in our backyard. I would sit on a little board, pretending it was a bench, and just think. I could hear my father snoring. He worked all night at the factory and went to bed just before dawn.

I loved my brothers. It wasn't that I didn't want to be near them. I just needed a place of my own.

121

I tiptoed around our tiny, two bedroom house. I peeked behind the curtain my mother had made from flour sacks to **separate** our living room from the **storage** closet.

"Aha! This is it! This could be my room." I imagined it with my own bed, table, and lamp—a place where I could read the books I loved, write in my diary, and dream.

I sat down among the boxes. My mother must have heard me because she came in from the kitchen.

> **Make and Confirm Predictions**
> What will the girl try to do with the storage closet?

"Mamá, it's perfect," I said, and I told her my idea.

"Ay, *mijita*, you do not understand. We are storing my sister's sewing machine and your uncle's garden tools. Someday they will need their things to make a better living in this new country. And there's the furniture and old clothes," she said. Slowly she shook her head.

123

Then she saw the **determination** on my face and the tears forming in my eyes. "Wait," she said, seriously thinking. "Maybe we could put these things on the back porch and cover them with old blankets."

"And we could put a tarp on top so nothing would get **ruined**," I added.

"Yes, I think we can do it. Let's take everything out and see how much space there is."

I gave her a great big hug and she kissed me.

After breakfast we started pushing the old furniture out to the back porch. Everyone helped. We were like a mighty team of powerful ants.

We carried furniture, tools, and machines. We dragged bulging bags of old clothes and toys. We pulled boxes of treasures and overflowing junk. Finally, everything was out except for a few cans of leftover paint from the one time we had painted the house.

Each can had just a tiny bit of paint inside. There was pink and blue and white, but not nearly enough of any one color to paint the room.

"I have an idea," I said to my brothers. "Let's mix them!" Héctor and Sergio helped me pour one can into another and we watched the colors swirl together. A new color began to appear, a little like purple and much stronger than pink. Magenta!

We painted and painted until we ran out of paint.

Mamá showed me how to measure my new magenta wall with a piece of bright yellow yarn left over from the last baby blanket she had crocheted. Tío Pancho was going back to Mexico and said I could have his bed, but we had to let him know if it would fit.

We cut off the piece of yarn that showed us just how big the bed could be. We all ran to Tío Pancho's waving the piece of yarn. We measured his bed. Perfect! That yellow piece of yarn was magical.

A little later Tío Pancho arrived with my new bed tied to the roof of his car. I ran out and hugged him. Papá helped him carry the bed in and carefully ease it into place.

My brothers jumped up and down and everybody clapped. Then Raúl moved an empty wooden crate over to my new bed and stood it on end to make a bedside table.

"All you need now is a little lamp," my mother said.

She brought out a shoe box stuffed with Blue Chip stamps she had been collecting for years. Mamá and Papá got them for free when they bought food or gas. They were like little prizes that could be used as money at special stores. But before we could spend them, we had to paste them into special stamp books.

We licked and licked and pasted and pasted. When we were done, Papá drove us to the stamp store.

Make and Confirm Predictions
What will the girl do with the Blue Chip stamps?

I saw the lamp I wanted right away. It was as dainty as a beautiful ballerina, made of white ceramic glass with a shade that had ruffles around the top and bottom.

I shut my eyes. I was so excited yet so afraid we wouldn't have enough stamps to get it. Then I heard my mother's voice. "Yes, *mijita*. We have enough."

When we got home, I carefully set the new lamp on my bedside table. Then I lay on my new bed and stared at the ceiling, thinking. Something was still missing, the most important thing …

Books!

The next day I went to our public library and rushed home with my arms full of books, six to be **exact**. It was my lucky number because there were six children in my family.

That evening, I turned on my new lamp and read and read. My two littlest brothers, Mario and Víctor, stood in the doorway holding back the flour-sack curtain. I invited them in. They cuddled up on my new bed and I read them a story. Then we said goodnight and they went back to their room.

I felt like the **luckiest**, happiest little girl in the whole world. Everyone in our family had helped to make my wish come true. Before I could even turn out the light, I fell asleep peacefully under a blanket of books in my very own room.

Amada and Maya's Room

Author Amada Irma Pérez grew up in a family just like the one in this story. Because her parents were unable to get the family a bigger house, there was not much room for Amada and her five brothers. But they did give Amada and her brothers lots of love and encouraged them to study and work hard.

Another book by Amada Irma Pérez:
My Diary from Here to There/Mi diario de aquí hasta allá

Illustrator Maya Christina Gonzalez has always loved to draw and paint. She has also always been very proud of being Mexican. In fact, as a child, Maya would draw her face on the blank page in the back of books because she wanted someone in the books to look like her.

LOG ON ▶ Find out more about Amada Irma Pérez and Maya Christina Gonzalez at **www.macmillanmh.com**.

CA Author's Purpose

What was the author's purpose for writing *My Very Own Room*? Did Amada Irma Pérez want to entertain or inform? Use details from the story in your answer.

Critical Thinking

Retell the Story

Use your Predictions Chart to help you retell *My Very Own Room*. Tell about events in the story that you predicted and then tell what actually happens.

What I Predict	What Happens

Think and Compare

1. What story details help you **predict** whether the girl will get a room of her own? Use your Predictions Chart to help you answer. **Monitor Comprehension: Make and Confirm Predictions**

2. Reread pages 119–123 of *My Very Own Room*. What kind of relationship does the girl have with her family? How do you know? Use story details to support your answer. **Analyze**

3. What are some reasons why you might want a quiet space of your own? **Evaluate**

4. Why is it good for a whole family to help one family member with a problem? **Apply**

5. Reread "Pond Street Clubhouse" on pages 114–115. Think about how the main character is like the girl in *My Very Own Room*. Why is **determination** an important character trait in both characters? **Reading/Writing Across Texts**

FRANK LLOYD WRIGHT

by Karen O'Malley

Frank Lloyd Wright was one of America's most famous architects. His building designs **influenced**, or had an effect on, many other architects. Wright's buildings include homes, office buildings, and one of the most famous museums in the world, the Guggenheim Museum in New York City. Frank Lloyd Wright believed that a building's **form**, or how it looks, should match its **function**, or how it is used.

Early Years

Wright was born in Wisconsin in 1867. When he was young, his mother gave him a set of wooden blocks, which helped him learn about **geometric** shapes, such as cubes, spheres, and cylinders. He also noticed the same shapes in nature. Wright went to the University of Wisconsin and then moved to Chicago to find work as an architect.

The Johnson Wax Company Building has many geometric shapes.

The Prairie Style

Frank Lloyd Wright believed that buildings should fit the places where they are built. The prairie style homes he built in the 1800s and early 1900s had low, straight lines that blended in with the prairie land where they stood.

The 1930s

In the 1930s Wright worked with architecture students who wanted to build the way he did. He designed one of his most famous houses, *Fallingwater*, in Pennsylvania. *Fallingwater* was built over a waterfall. During the 1930s Wright also designed the Johnson Wax Company Building in Wisconsin.

Fallingwater in Bear Run, Pennsylvania

An Encyclopedia Article

Reading an Encyclopedia Article

Encyclopedia articles are arranged alphabetically in each volume, or book.

page number   **guide word**   **caption**

503   Architecture

heading →

Architecture

Architecture is the art of designing buildings. An architect is a person who designs buildings and checks to make sure they are built correctly. Architects build many different kinds of buildings, including homes, schools, office buildings, skyscrapers, and monuments.

The Guggenheim Museum was designed by the architect Frank Lloyd Wright (1867-1959).

Early Architecture

Architecture began when people built the first homes. The architecture of the ancient Egyptians included giant pyramids that were built for kings. Ancient Greeks were known for the beautiful stone columns of their early temples and monuments.

This article is from Volume A of an encyclopedia.

Later Years

Wright designed both the Guggenheim Museum in New York City and the Marin County Civic Center in California at the end of his career. He died in Arizona in 1959 before either of the buildings opened.

The ideas and work of Frank Lloyd Wright are **preserved**, or kept, by The Frank Lloyd Wright Foundation. The Foundation watches over his designs, drawings, writings, and his homes in Arizona and Wisconsin.

The Frank Lloyd Wright Foundation is located in Arizona.

 Critical Thinking

1. Look at the encyclopedia article on Architecture on page 142. What do you think the numbers in parentheses mean? **Reading an Encyclopedia Article**

2. If you could travel back to the early 1900s to meet Frank Lloyd Wright, what questions would you ask him? **Apply**

3. Think about this article and *My Very Own Room*. Why might the narrator of the story enjoy learning about Frank Lloyd Wright? **Reading/Writing Across Texts**

 History/Social Science Activity

Find out more about a famous building such as the Eiffel Tower or the Sydney Opera House. Find out who the architect was and when the building was built.

 Find out more about architecture at **www.macmillanmh.com**.

Focus on Object

Good writers use strong details and descriptive words to **focus on object**.

Reading and Writing Connection

Read the passage below. Notice how author Amada Irma Pérez focuses on an object, in this case, a crowded bed.

The author focuses in on the brothers' positions on the bed. We are able to picture the scene through the use of specific details.

I woke up one morning on a crowded bed in a crowded room. Victor's elbow was jabbing me in the ribs. Mario had climbed out of his crib and crawled in with us. Now his leg lay across my face and I could hardly breathe.

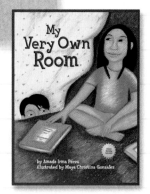

My Very Own Room

by Amada Irma Pérez
illustrated by Maya Christina Gonzalez

Read and Find

Read Max's writing below. What did he do to focus on the object? Use the tips below to help you.

Taking Care of Layla
by Max G.

When my friend was in the hospital, I helped take care of her dog, Layla. Boy, was she a project! She loved to dig through the garbage, tearing apart my microwave popcorn bag to eat the butter and unpopped kernels. She was in dog heaven in the mud puddle in our backyard, which she rolled around in every chance she had.

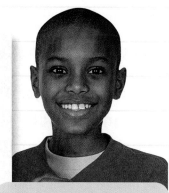

Read about my dogsitting experience.

Writer's Checklist

☑ Did the writer write about one **object**?

☑ Did the writer include specific details about that object?

☑ Can the reader picture the object the way Max experienced it?

Evan's Welcome

One morning at Northside School, a friendly woman greeted children in the front hallway. Right before classes began, a shy boy walked up to her. She asked the boy his name.

"My name is Evan," he replied as he looked at the ground.

The woman smiled and said, "Welcome to Northside. I'm the principal, Mrs. Bordoni."

"Good morning," said Evan, looking sad.

"I know you are new, but you will like it here," said Mrs. Bordoni. "I will show you the way to your new classroom."

"I didn't want to move … and leave my friends," whispered Evan.

Mrs. Bordoni responded, "I know. You will have friends here, too. You'll see."

She walked him to Room 106 and introduced him to his teacher, Mr. Cortez.

"Welcome to our class," said Mr. Cortez. "We were talking about a story we just read. Who can tell Evan what it was about?"

One of the girls raised her hand and answered, "This family moves to a new state. It's a funny and sad story."

Evan seemed to cheer up a bit. He asked, "Did they like the new place?"

Marco answered, "Not at first. But by the end, they made lots of new friends."

Tom added, "The girl from next door said she needed help. When they got to her house, there was a party and a sign that read *Welcome!*"

"The neighbors really made the family feel welcome," Mr. Cortez stated.

Later, Mrs. Bordoni returned to walk Evan to lunch. As they entered the lunchroom, Evan spotted a sign inside reading *Welcome Evan!*

Evan smiled. "I can't believe you did this for me," he said. Three students in costumes came in carrying a cake that read *Welcome Evan!* Evan asked, "Why are the kids dressed in costumes?"

Mr. Cortez answered, "They are characters in a play. I believe they still need another cat."

"Could I be the cat?" asked Evan.

"That's exactly what we were hoping. That way you'll fit right in!" answered Mrs. Bordoni.

Evan cried, "That's great! My biggest fear was that I wouldn't fit in. Thanks!"

Mrs. Bordoni responded, "You're welcome. Now let's eat the cake!"

Snakes!

When you think of a rattle, you probably picture a cute baby toy. However, there is another type of rattle that no one should play with. This is the kind of rattle that you find on a rattlesnake's tail.

Many different kinds of rattlesnakes live in the United States. They live as far north as Maine and Washington State, and as far south as southern Florida. They come in different colors and designs. Most rattlesnakes eat small rodents or lizards. Some types of rattlesnakes can grow to be seven feet long!

If you're on a walk in the desert and you hear a rattle, get moving. The rattler may bite you! Luckily, you probably

A rattlesnake forms a new rattle each time it sheds its skin.

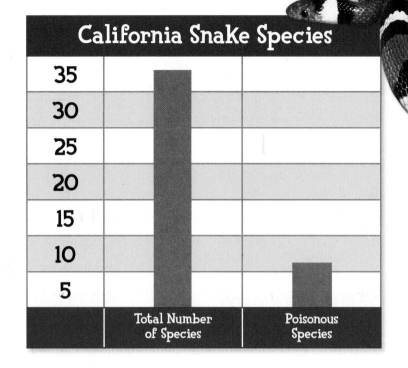

California Snake Species

	Total Number of Species	Poisonous Species
35		
30		
25		
20		
15		
10		
5		

All of California's poisonous snakes are rattlesnakes. Rattlesnake species include the sidewinder and the Mohave rattlesnake.

will never meet a rattlesnake. Rattlers try to avoid humans. In fact, these snakes only attack us if they feel cornered. When a rattlesnake thinks it is in danger, it shakes its tail, or rattle. The noise is a warning sign for others to go away!

Rattlesnakes are only one type of snake. Around the world, there are about 3,000 species of snakes. Unlike rattlesnakes, most are not poisonous. However, even nonpoisonous snakes can be harmful to other animals. Some snakes, such as boa

constrictors, are dangerous in other ways. Boa constrictors wind around their prey and squeeze until their prey stops breathing. Other snakes swallow small animals whole.

Snakes have good qualities, too! For example, snakes eat many rats and mice. Rats and mice can spread diseases to humans. If there were no snakes, many more people could get sick from diseases spread by these rodents. So next time you see a snake, remember to respect its qualities, both good and bad!

CA Critical Thinking

Now answer numbers 1 through 4. Base your answers on the passage "Evan's Welcome."

1. **The SETTINGS in this passage are**

    A   a car, a classroom, and a lunchroom.

    B   Evan's house and his new school.

    C   Evan's old school and his new school.

    D   a school hallway, a classroom, and a lunchroom.

2. **What happens at the END of the story?**

    A   Evan is excited to be in a play with the other students.

    B   Evan feels like he doesn't fit in, and wishes he were back in his old school.

    C   The principal greets Evan.

    D   His new classmates tell him about a story they read.

3. **What CAUSES Evan to cheer up a bit in the middle of the passage?**

    A   He sees someone he knows from his old school.

    B   His mom comes to pick him up early.

    C   He is interested in the story that the class has just read.

    D   He gets to eat cake.

4. **How does the principal, Mrs. Bordoni, try to make Evan feel welcome? Use DETAILS and information from the passage to support your answer.**

Now answer numbers 1 through 4. Base your answers on the article "Snakes!"

1. **When might a rattlesnake shake its tail?**

   A   When it goes to sleep.
   B   When it sees a bird.
   C   When it wants to warn another animal.
   D   When it recognizes another snake.

2. **According to the bar graph, about how many species of snakes in California are poisonous?**

   A   50   B   33
   C   6   D   None

3. **Read these sentences from paragraph 4 of the article.**

   > Unlike rattlesnakes, most are not poisonous. However, even <u>nonpoisonous</u> snakes can be harmful to other animals.

   In the sentences above, the PREFIX <u>non-</u> means

   A   not   B   very
   C   against   D   again

4. **What is one positive EFFECT snakes have on humans?**

   A   They fertilize soil, which helps farmland.
   B   They eat rodents, which helps stop the spread of disease.
   C   They entertain us with their dancing.
   D   Their venom makes tasty drinks.

Write on Demand

PROMPT Should people fear snakes? Why or why not? Use details from the article to support your answer. Write for 5 minutes. Write as much as you can, as well as you can.

The **Big** Question

How do community members work together?

Theme Launcher Video

LOG ON ▶ Find out more about how community members work together at www.macmillanmh.com.

How do community members work together?

A community is a place where people live, work, and play. In order for communities to survive and grow, people need to work together. Communities need mail carriers, police officers, firefighters, and bus drivers. They need doctors, garbage collectors, and teachers. They also need volunteers—people who help others without getting paid.

Some California communities began with the Gold Rush of 1849. Then more people settled, looking for gold, building businesses, and building homes. That's how we have many California communities today!

Research Activities

In this unit you will read about how people help their communities. Research your community. Write about its history and the people who have helped it grow.

Keep Track of Ideas

As you read, keep track of all you learn about how community members work together. Use the Accordion Book organizer. Label the first section, "Neighborhoods and Communities." Use a different section for each week. Write what you learn each week.

FOLDABLES®
Study Organizer

Unit Theme | Week 1 | Week 2 | Week 3 | Week 4 | Week 5

Research Toolkit

Conduct Your Unit 2 Research Online with:

Research Roadmap
Follow step-by-step guide to complete your research project.

Online Resources
- Topic Finder and other Research Tools
- Videos and Virtual Fieldtrips
- Photos and Drawings for Presentations
- Related Articles and Web Resources

California Web Site Links

LOG ON ▶ Go to **www.macmillanmh.com** for more information.

California People

Robina Suwol, Environmentalist and Community Activist

Robina Suwol works to make schools safe for students, teachers, school employees, and visitors.

Birth of a Town

CA **Talk About It**

How are communities created? What do they need to grow?

LOG ON Find out more about the birth of a town at www.macmillanmh.com.

157

Let's Trade!

by Alex Ely

Vocabulary

sidewalks   blossomed

grumbled   wailed

traders   lonesome

Word Parts

Compound Words are words that are made up of two smaller words.

side + walks = *sidewalks*

Elizabeth and Danny walked along newly paved **sidewalks** on a frosty winter morning. Elizabeth wore a hat and gloves but no scarf. Danny wore a hat and two scarves, but he didn't have any gloves. Both of them were freezing.

"I'm so cold," Elizabeth **grumbled** under her breath.

"Me, too," Danny **wailed**.

Then Elizabeth had an idea! "What if I traded you one glove for one of your scarves?" Elizabeth said. "Then both of our necks would be warm, and we'd each have one warm hand. We could put the other hand in our pockets."

"Good idea!" said Danny.

After they shared the scarf and glove, they began to feel warmer.

A few minutes later Mrs. Baxter appeared. "Did I just see you barter?" she asked.

Elizabeth and Danny looked puzzled. "What's barter?" Elizabeth asked.

"Barter means trade," Mrs. Baxter explained. "You two traded a scarf and a glove so you could be warm. Did you know that **traders** bartered for thousands of years?"

"Really? How?" Danny asked.

Mrs. Baxter said, "Well, traders who had too much of one thing, such as salt or pigs, would exchange with other traders for things that they needed. Trading grew and **blossomed**, but it had problems."

"Like what?" Elizabeth asked.

"Suppose you raised chickens. You could trade the chickens and eggs for what you needed. But if the chickens got away—"

"I wouldn't have anything to trade!"

"Exactly!" said Mrs. Baxter.

"And you'd be so **lonesome** without your poultry friends!" Danny said with a grin.

"Now you see why people began to use money to trade," Mrs. Baxter said.

"Is it true that silver and gold coins were used before paper money?" Danny asked.

"Yes, but they were too heavy to carry." Mrs. Baxter said. "People then began to write promises on paper instead of trading coins. That was how paper money got its start."

"Wow!" said Elizabeth, "but I guess people still trade sometimes, the way Danny and I did today!"

Reread for Comprehension

Summarize

Sequence The **sequence** in a story is the order in which events take place. Knowing the sequence of events will help you better understand a story. You can summarize a story by paying close attention to the order in which the events happen. Reread the selection. Use your Sequence Chart to record the story's events in time order.

Event

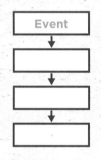

CA Comprehension

Genre

Historical Fiction is a story in which fictional characters take part in real events from the past.

Summarize

Sequence

As you read, use your Sequence Chart.

Event

Read to Find Out

How does Amanda help her town become a boom town?

BOOM TOWN

By Sonia Levitin

Illustrated by Cat Bowman Smith

Award Winning Author

It took us twenty-one days on the stagecoach to get to California. When we got there, I thought we'd live with Pa in the gold fields. A whole tent city was built up. But Ma shook her head. "The gold fields are no place for children. We'll get a cabin and live in town."

What town? A stage stop, a pump house, a few log cabins— that was all. It was so wide and **lonesome** out west, even my shadow ran off.

Ma found a cabin big enough for all of us: Baby
Betsy, brothers Billy, Joe, Ted, and me—Amanda.
Pa came in from the gold fields every Saturday night,
singing:

"So I got me a mule
And some mining tools,
A shovel and a pick and a pan;

But I work all day
Without no pay.
I guess I'm a foolish man."

First Ma made him take a bath in a tin tub set out
under the stars. Then Pa sang songs and told stories
he'd heard from the miners—stories about men
finding big nuggets and striking it rich. But poor Pa,
he had no luck at all. Still, every Monday morning
he'd leave for the gold fields full of hope.

Days were long and lonely. The hills spread out as far as forever. Nights, me and Ma and my brothers and Baby Betsy would sit out and wait for a shooting star to sail across the sky. Once in a while a crow flew by. That's all the excitement there was.

My brothers worked up some furrows. They planted corn and potatoes and beans. Then they ran around climbing trees, skinning their knees. But after all the water was fetched and the wash was done, after the soap was made and the fire laid, after the beds were fixed and the floor was swept clean, I'd sit outside our cabin door with Baby Betsy, so bored I thought I'd die. Also, I hankered for some pie. I loved to bake pie.

I asked Ma and she said, "Pie would be good, but we have no pie pans and no real oven, just the wood stove. How would you bake a pie?"

I poked around in a big box of stuff and found an old iron skillet. I decided to make a pie crust and pick gooseberries to fill it.

Gooseberries grew on the bushes near town. I picked a big pailful and went back home. I made a crust with flour, butter, a little water, and a pinch of salt, and then I rolled it out.

Ma came in and said, "Looks good, Amanda. I knew you could make it. But tell me, how will you bake it?"

I showed Ma the skillet. She shook her head. "I don't think it will work, but you can try."

"It will work," I said.

> **Sequence**
> What steps does Amanda take to start baking her pie?

Brothers Billy and Joe and Ted stood there laughing. When the wood turned to coals, I pushed my pie inside the old stove. After a while I smelled a bad burning. I pulled out my pie, hard as a rock. Billy, Joe, and Ted whooped and slapped their sides. They snatched up my pie and tossed it high into the air. They ran outside and Billy whacked it hard with a stick. Pie pieces flew all over the place, and my brothers bent over, laughing.

I was so mad I went right back in to make another, and I swore none of them would get a bite. I rolled out my crust and filled it with berries, shoved the pie into the oven, and soon took it out.

I set the pie down to cool. I went off to do some mending. Next thing I knew, Baby Betsy, just learning to walk, sat there with pie goo all over her face. Too soft, the filling ran down on Betsy, and she **wailed** like a coyote in the night.

It took one more try, but I got it right. That night we ate my gooseberry pie, and it was delicious.

When Pa came home from the gold fields on Saturday night, there was a pie for him, too. "Amanda, you are the queen of the kitchen!" Pa scooped me up and whirled me around. I was proud.

The next week I made an extra pie for Pa to take with him to the gold fields.

Saturday night when he came home singing, coins jangled in his pocket.

We all ran out to ask, "Did you strike gold, Pa?"

"No," he said. "I sold Amanda's pie. The miners loved it. They paid me twenty-five cents a slice!"

After that, Pa took pies to the gold fields every week. And every week he came home with coins in his pockets. Some miners walked right to our door looking for pie. They told Ma, "You should open a bakery."

Ma said, "It's my girl Amanda who is the baker. If she wants to make pies, that's fine. But I have no time."

Ma had a new baby on the way. It was up to me. I figured I could sell pies to the miners and fill up our money jar.

But I needed help. I rounded up my brothers and told them, "If you want to eat pie, you've got to work."

They **grumbled** and groaned, but they knew I meant it. So Billy built me a shelf, Joe made a sign, AMANDA'S FINE PIES, and Ted helped pick berries and sour apples.

I needed more pans and another bucket. One day Peddler Pete came by, and with the money I'd made I bought them.

"You're a right smart little girl," said the peddler, "being in business like this."

I thought fast and told him, "Anybody can make money out here. Folks need things all the time, and there're no stores around. If you were to settle and start one, I'll bet you'd get rich."

Peddler Pete scratched his beard. "Not a bad idea," he said. "My feet are sore from roaming. I could use this cart and build my way up to having a store."

So pretty soon we had us a real store called PEDDLER PETE'S TRADING POST. Trappers and **traders** and travelers appeared. After shopping at Pete's, they were good and hungry.

They came to our cabin, looking for pie. Some liked it here so well they decided to stay. Soon we had a cooper, a tanner, a miller, a blacksmith. A town was starting to grow.

A prospector came in on the stage from St. Joe, his clothes covered with dirt. He looked around at the folks eating pie, and he asked, "Is there someone here who does washing?"

I stepped right up and I told him, "What we need is a laundry. Why don't you stay and start one? Why, the miners are sending their shirts clear to China. You'll make more money doing laundry than looking for gold."

The man thought a while, then said with a smile, "You're right, little lady. It's a dandy idea. I'll send for my wife to help."

Soon shirts and sheets fluttered on the line as people brought their washing in. A tailor came to make and mend clothes. A cobbler crafted shoes and boots. We heard the *tap tap* of his hammer and smelled the sweet leather. A barber moved in with shaving mugs, and an apothecary with herbs and healing drugs. So the town grew up all around us.

My pie business **blossomed**. Sometimes the line snaked clear around the house. Baby Betsy entertained the people while they waited. Billy added another shelf. Joe and Ted made a bench. We all picked berries and apples. Even Ma came to help. We had to get a bigger jar for all the money coming in.

One day our old friend Cowboy Charlie rode by. Like everyone else, he stopped for some pie. "I'd like to rest a spell," he said. "Where can I leave my horse for the night?"

"There's no livery stable," I said. "But why don't you start one? You'd rent out horses, and wagons too. That would be the perfect business for you."

"You're just full of great ideas, little lady," Cowboy Charlie said. He twirled his lariat. "I'd like to settle down. I'll stay here and do just that."

Soon a trail was worn right to Charlie's stable door. All day we heard the snorting of horses. Now Charlie needed hay. Farmers brought wagons and sacks full of feed. With all those people riding in, someone decided to build a hotel and a cafe. The town grew fast all around us.

The owner of the cafe bought pies from me, five or six at a time. I taught Billy how to roll the crust. Joe got wood for the stove. Ted washed the fruit, and Baby Betsy tried to stir in the sugar.

The money jar in our kitchen looked ready to bust. Where could we safely keep all that cash? Lucky us, one day Mr. Hooper, the banker, appeared.

"I'm building a bank," Mr. Hooper said to me. "This is getting to be a boom town."

"We'll use your bank," I told Mr. Hooper, "but the roads are so poor. In winter there's mud, and in summer there's dust. We need some **sidewalks** and better streets."

"You're a smart little lady," said Mr. Hooper, tipping his hat. "I'll see what I can do about that."

Before we knew it, the bank was built and wooden sidewalks were laid. One street was called Bank Street; the other was Main. Soon every lane and landmark had a name. Pa and my brothers built on a big room for our bakery.

Men sent for their families. New houses appeared everywhere. Babies and children filled up the town. We needed a school, and a good schoolmarm.

We knew Miss Camilla from our stagecoach days. She was living up the coast a ways. Cowboy Charlie rode off to fetch her, and she was glad to come.

Miss Camilla, the teacher, had married a preacher, and he came too. We all got together to build a church and a school. Bells rang out every day of the week. Now this was a real boom town!

One day Pa said to me, "Amanda, I'm through panning for gold. Will you let me be in business with you?"

"Sure!" I said, happily. "I'd love to work with you, Pa, and I'd also like to go to school."

Sequence
What sequence of events takes place to create this boom town?

So Pa turned to baking, and we all worked together.
Pa sang while he rolled out the dough:

"Amanda found a skillet
And berries to fill it,
Made pies without a pan;

Our pies are the best
In all the West.
I guess I'm a lucky man."

Now Pa is with us every day. There's excitement
and bustle all around. Our house sits in the middle of
a boom town!

And to think it all started with me, Amanda, baking pies!

BANK ON SONIA AND CAT

AUTHOR
Sonia Levitin wrote this story after reading about a woman who made more than $10,000 by baking pies in a skillet during the California Gold Rush. Sonia loves research, so it is not surprising that she found such an interesting fact. History is just one of the things that Sonia likes to write about. She also writes mysteries, adventures, and funny stories.

ILLUSTRATOR
Cat Bowman Smith started out drawing magazine pictures. Her illustrations became very popular. Soon she was illustrating books. Today she has illustrated more than 40 of them.

LOG ON ▶ Find out more about Sonia Levitin and Cat Bowman Smith at **www.macmillanmh.com**.

Other books by Sonia Levitin: *Nine for California* and *Taking Charge*

CA ## Author's Purpose
Did Sonia Levitin write to entertain or to inform? What clues help you figure out her purpose?

CA Critical Thinking

Summarize

Use your Sequence Chart to help you summarize *Boom Town*. Retell the story's events in the sequence in which they happen.

Event
↓
↓
↓

Think and Compare

1. Describe two events that happened after Amanda's pie business **blossomed**. Tell them in the proper **sequence**. Use details in your answer. **Summarize: Sequence**

2. Reread pages 168–169 of *Boom Town*. What do these pages show about Amanda's character? Use specific details to support your answer. **Analyze**

3. Suppose you wanted to start your own business. What information from the story could help you to be successful? Explain. **Apply**

4. Why are new businesses important to the growth of a town or a city? Use examples from the story to support your ideas. **Evaluate**

5. Read "Let's Trade!" on pages 158–159. Compare how characters in "Let's Trade!" and *Boom Town* get the things they need. **Reading/Writing Across Texts**

How to Earn Money!

by R. J. Harkin

Would you like to do something new and exciting? Would you like to be looked up to and respected by kids and adults alike? Would you like to earn money in your free time? If you answered "Yes!" to any of these questions, then starting your own **business** might be right for you!

You Can Do It!

"My own business?" you might ask. "But I'm only a third-grader!" No problem! Even third-graders have plenty of talent and **services** to offer.

Do you enjoy cooking or baking? Then you may consider whipping up and selling a few **batches** of your fabulous blueberry muffins. Do you like arts and crafts? If so, you can make and sell artwork or jewelry. Do animals like you? Many busy families need responsible people to walk their dogs and feed their cats. The possibilities are endless! So, wash a car, plant a garden, or rake a lawn. If people want and need your special talents and services, you'll soon be in business!

Starting a Dog-Washing Business

Using a Calendar

A calendar is a kind of chart that organizes information in chronological order. A calendar can help you keep track of what you need to do.

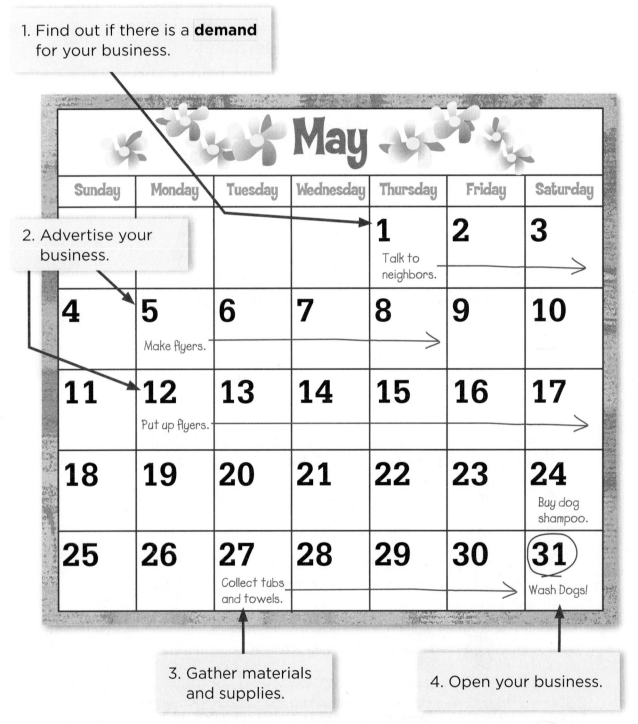

1. Find out if there is a **demand** for your business.

2. Advertise your business.

May

Sunday	Monday	Tuesday	Wednesday	Thursday	Friday	Saturday
				1 Talk to neighbors.	2	3 →
4	5 Make flyers.	6	7 →	8	9	10
11	12 Put up flyers.	13	14	15	16	17 →
18	19	20	21	22	23	24 Buy dog shampoo.
25	26	27 Collect tubs and towels.	28	29	30 →	(31) Wash Dogs!

3. Gather materials and supplies.

4. Open your business.

 Critical Thinking

1. Look at the calendar on page 186. Which days are used for advertising? How will this be done? **Using a Calendar**

2. Suppose you live in a neighborhood where most people work all day. Many people are not home to cook, work in the yard, or spend time with their pets. What businesses might people want to use? **Apply**

3. What advice do you think Amanda could give kids who want to start a business today? **Reading/Writing Across Texts**

 History/Social Science Activity

Research a business that interests you. Create a calendar that shows your preparations for opening that business.

 Find out more about businesses at **www.macmillanmh.com**.

Writing

CA

✔ Showing

Include details in your writing that **show** your reader a strong image of what you are writing about.

Read the passage below. Notice how author Sonia Levitin shows a moment in her story.

An excerpt from
Boom Town

The author shows us the moment when Amanda takes out her first pie. She shows us exactly how that pie turned out and what the family did with it.

I pulled out my pie, hard as a rock. Billy, Joe, and Ted whooped and slapped their sides. They snatched up my pie and tossed it high into the air. They ran outside and Billy whacked it hard with a stick. Pie pieces flew all over the place, and my brothers bent over, laughing.

Read and Find

Read Lola's writing below. What did she do to help show you the moment? Use the tips below to help you.

Tag!
by Lola L.

I spun around and ran after Miguel. He zig-zagged across the playground, just out of my reach. My legs were pushing as hard as possible. I could hear myself breathing heavily. I leaned forward to make my arm reach further. "Tag!" I yelled as my fingers tapped his shoulder.

Read about my game of tag.

Writer's Checklist

✓ Does the writer include details about how people felt and moved?

✓ Does the writer describe how the moment looked and sounded?

☑ Does Lola **show** you the moment as though you were seeing it through her eyes?

Starting a
Local
Business

Why is it important for a community to support its local businesses?

LOG ON Find out more about local businesses at **www.macmillanmh.com**.

FRESH CABBAGE
~~1$~~ per EA.
0.75 ¢ per EA

ROMA TOMATOES
50¢/pound
no sprays!

75¢

Save Our Butterflies

by Sean Bryant

Scientists who study insects believe that something is happening to our butterflies. They say that 30 years ago, there were about twice as many butterflies as there are today. Where have all the butterflies gone?

The Problem

No one hurts butterflies on purpose. Still, scientists think that people have caused the butterfly problem. Butterflies find their food in wildflowers. When people clear the land for roads and buildings, these flowers **disappear**.

Some insects eat and destroy farmers' crops. Farmers use pesticides, or poisons, to get rid of harmful insects. Pesticides **protect** crops, but sometimes end up **harming** helpful insects such as caterpillars. Caterpillars turn into butterflies. This is another reason there are fewer butterflies now than in the past.

How to Help

Luckily, there are ways that kids and grownups can help. Do you want to get involved and help save our butterflies?

One thing you can do is plant a garden. Make sure the garden has a good **supply** of the food butterflies eat when they are caterpillars. Different kinds of caterpillars eat different plants. Monarch butterfly caterpillars eat milkweed. Black swallowtail caterpillars eat parsley, dill, or carrot leaves. Find out what kind of butterflies live in your area and plant the kinds of food they eat as caterpillars. Make sure that pesticides are not used nearby.

One More Thing

Some kids like to **capture** butterflies with nets. Then they put them in a jar or other **enclosure**. Unfortunately, it is easy to hurt a butterfly when you catch it. Its wings are torn easily. Instead, enjoy these beautiful insects from a distance.

Reread for **Comprehension**

Monitor Comprehension

Draw Conclusions Sometimes readers need to **draw conclusions** about, or figure out, what an author means in a story. By monitoring your comprehension in this way, you will better understand what you read.

To draw conclusions, use details from the story and what you know. Reread the selection. Use your Conclusion Map to record clues. Draw a conclusion about butterflies.

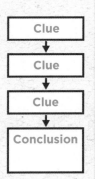

Clue
Clue
Clue
Conclusion

193

CA Comprehension

Genre
Nonfiction gives information about real people, places, or things.

Monitor Comprehension

Draw Conclusions
As you read, use your Conclusion Map.

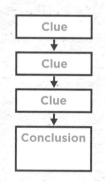

```
┌──────────┐
│   Clue   │
└──────────┘
     ↓
┌──────────┐
│   Clue   │
└──────────┘
     ↓
┌──────────┐
│   Clue   │
└──────────┘
     ↓
┌──────────┐
│Conclusion│
│          │
└──────────┘
```

Read to Find Out
How have butterflies helped the community?

194

HOME-GROWN
BUTTERFLIES

by Deborah Churchman

People in Barra del Colorado, a village in Costa Rica, had a big problem. For many years, the villagers had caught fish for a living. But then, because of pollution and overfishing, the fish began to **disappear**. Soon it became hard for the people to catch enough fish to feed to their families and sell for money. What could they do?

The village is on the edge of a beautiful rainforest. One thing the villagers could have done was chop down the trees. Then they could have sold the wood and farmed the land. They would have made money but destroyed the rainforest.

A scientist named Brent Davies had another idea about how the villagers could use the rainforest. And it would keep the forest alive. The villagers could raise and sell *butterflies*.

◀ **School children in Barra del Colorado are now experts at spotting caterpillars.**

▼ **Brent Davies and local students admire a sign that notes—in Spanish and English—they are raising insects.**

FINQUITA DE MARIPOSAS
DESARROLLO SOSTENIBLE
EN EDUCACIÓN A LOS NIÑOS
BUTTERFLY FARM PROJECT
OF BARRA del COLORADO

Many colorful butterflies flit around in the forest near Barra del Colorado. It would be easy to **capture** a few and use them to raise many more.

Brent knew that butterfly zoos around the world would pay for farm-raised butterflies. If the villagers could make money by selling them, they'd have a good reason to **protect** the insects' rainforest home. After all, without the forest, there would be no wild butterflies to capture. And without a steady **supply** of wild butterflies, the farm would fail.

Brent wanted to show villagers how to raise butterflies to sell. And she knew just who could help: the school kids! If adults saw kids making money with butterflies, they might want to start their own farm—and protect the forest.

Draw Conclusions
What kind of person is Brent Davies? How do you know?

Schoolyard Farm

Butterflies drink nectar from certain flowers, and they lay their eggs on other plants. When the eggs hatch, caterpillars come out and eat those plants. They eat and grow, and grow and eat. When they've grown enough, the caterpillars turn into pupae (PEW-pee). And those are what butterfly zoos buy.

Brent knew that villagers could find some pupae in the rainforest to sell. But if the people could get butterflies to lay eggs in one place, they could *raise* caterpillars—and get many more pupae.

They could even let some of the extra butterflies they raised go free in the rainforest. That would make sure the forest would always have plenty.

So, how to get started? To attract butterflies, Brent figured the villagers needed a garden full of nectar plants. They also needed an **enclosure** full of plants for caterpillars to eat. She talked to people at the school. Together they decided on a good spot in the schoolyard.

Inside an enclosed area, visitors can see plants grown for hungry caterpillars.

CLEARING AND PLANTING

First they had to clear a lot of trash out of the schoolyard. The kids pitched in and stuffed more than 100 sacks with trash. Soon people were stopping by to admire their work.

Then everyone helped dig up the soil so that plants could grow. That turned up lots of worms—which attracted lots of chickens. So the kids went on "chicken patrol," chasing the birds away. Their butterfly garden needed those worms!

Next, they planted flowers to attract the butterflies. Beside the flower garden, they built the enclosure for raising caterpillars. Then they put the right kinds of plants inside it.

199

RAISING BUTTERFLIES

Butterflies from the forest flew to the garden to feed on the flowers. Brent taught the children how to capture the butterflies and take them into the enclosure. There, the butterflies laid tiny eggs on the special plants.

Brent also taught the children how to find caterpillars and eggs. (Some eggs are no bigger than the period at the end of this sentence.)

The kids learned to lift up leaves and look around the plants. They put the eggs and caterpillars they found into special feeding boxes. That way they could make sure the insects got plenty to eat.

Draw Conclusions
Why is it important for the kids to find as many eggs and caterpillars as possible?

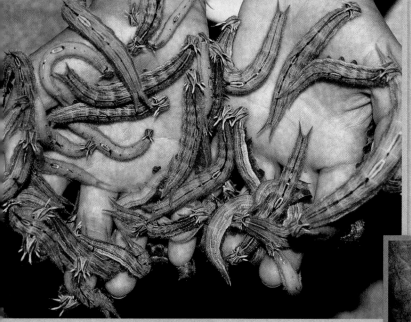

◄ **Two handfuls of owl butterfly caterpillars are moved to a feeding box.**

After caterpillars turn into pupae, they are ▶ **packed into boxes and shipped to zoos.**

Blue morpho butterflies are bestsellers. Their wings have "eyespots" on the underside, but the topside is bright blue.

In the boxes, the caterpillars fattened up on leaves. Then they turned into pupae. The kids picked the pupae just as if they were picking a crop. They let some of the pupae turn into butterflies, and they put those back into the rainforest. But they sold the other pupae.

Today, the farm sells about 250 pupae every month. The money that's earned goes to the school for materials and equipment. The first thing the kids bought was a ceiling fan so their schoolroom wouldn't be so hot!

The best news is that some adults in the village have started doing what the kids have done—making farms for butterflies. They've learned from the kids how to use the forest without **harming** it.

The bottom blue morpho butterfly has just crawled out of its pupae case. The top one has been out for half an hour.

Kids in San Pasqual, California, gather eggs from plants outside their butterfly farm's enclosure.

MEANWHILE, BACK HOME

People at the San Diego Wild Animal Park helped start the butterfly farm in Costa Rica. Then they had another wild idea. Why not start this kind of farm at home in California?

They asked students at San Pasqual Union Elementary School if they wanted to get involved. People at the school agreed to do the same thing as the villagers in Costa Rica.

Kids and adults set up a butterfly garden and an enclosed area. Some of the money they earn pays for special things for their school, such as science equipment.

Students from California have started writing to the students in Costa Rica about their butterfly businesses. Both groups of kids feel great about what they're doing for nature!

Charlie Hanscom is just one of the kids raising money for San Pasqual Union Elementary School by helping with the butterfly farm.

FLY AWAY WITH DEBORAH

REPORTER

DEBORAH CHURCHMAN grew up next to a creek in the suburbs near Washington, D.C. Now she grows butterfly bushes and other wildlife-attracting plants in her yard for the enjoyment of her four kids and granddaughter. Deborah is a senior editor at *Ranger Rick*, where she writes articles about nature every day.

LOG ON ▶ Find out more about Deborah Churchman at **www.macmillanmh.com**.

CA Author's Purpose

What was Deborah Churchman's purpose for writing *Home-Grown Butterflies*? Did she want to inform readers about butterflies or to persuade readers to grow them? How do you know?

CA Critical Thinking

Summarize

Use your Conclusion Map to help you summarize *Home-Grown Butterflies.* Explain how the children were able to help their community by growing butterflies.

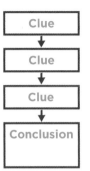

Think and Compare

1. **Draw a conclusion** about how well Brent Davies's plan worked. Use your Conclusion Map and article details to answer. **Monitor Comprehension: Draw Conclusions**

2. Reread page 202. Why is it good that the California students write to the students in Costa Rica? Use information from the article in your answer. **Analyze**

3. What would you add to Brent Davies's plan to make it even more successful? **Apply**

4. The people of Barra del Colorado learned how to earn money without **harming** the rain forest. Why is this an important lesson? Explain your answer. **Evaluate**

5. Read "Save Our Butterflies" on pages 192–193. How is this selection similar to *Home-Grown Butterflies*? How are the two selections different? Use details from both selections in your answer. **Reading/Writing Across Texts**

Poetry

Free Verse Poems do not have any regular pattern of line length, rhyme, meter, or stanzas.

Rhyming Poems use elements such as rhyme and rhythm to express feelings and ideas.

✔ Literary Elements

Personification is when an animal or thing is given human characteristics in a poem or story.

Assonance is the repetition of the same or similar vowel sounds in a series of words.

> The butterfly talks like a person. It also thinks like a person. This is personification.

Monarch Butterfly

Wait I can wait
     For the fullness of wings
     For the lift   For the flight
Wait I can wait
     A moment less
     A moment more
I have waited much longer before
     For the taste of the flower
     For the feel   For the sight
Wait I can wait
     For the prize of the skies
     For the gift of the air
Almost finished
Almost there
     Almost ready
          to rise

— Marilyn Singer

The Caterpillar

Brown and furry
Caterpillar in a hurry,
Take your walk
To the shady leaf, or stalk,
Or what not,
Which may be the chosen spot.
No toad spy you,

Hovering bird of prey pass
by you;
Spin and die,
To live again a butterfly.

— *Christina Rossetti*

The words *chosen, No,* and *toad* repeat the long *o* sound to create assonance.

CA Critical Thinking

1. Find an example of assonance in "Monarch Butterfly." **Assonance**

2. How does the poet use personification in "Monarch Butterfly"? **Analyze**

3. Which stage of a butterfly's life is described in "Monarch Butterfly"? How did *Home-Grown Butterflies* help you figure this out? Use details from each selection in your answer. **Reading/Writing Across Texts**

LOG ON ▶ Find out more about poetry at **www.macmillanmh.com**.

Writing

CA

✓ **Showing**

When you **show** a moment in writing, be sure to include interesting details, words, and phrases that will add interest.

Read the passage below. Notice how author Deborah Churchman shows a moment in her story.

An excerpt from
Home-Grown Butterflies

The author shows us a funny moment from the children's project. She tries to include details about the moment that will make us giggle.

Then everyone helped dig up the soil so that plants could grow. That turned up lots of worms—which attracted lots of chickens. So the kids went on "chicken patrol," chasing the birds away. Their butterfly garden needed those worms!

Read and Find

Read Drew's writing below. What does she show you that helps you imagine the moment? Use the tips below to help you.

The Mistake
by Drew Z.

Crash! I looked down at the tiny pieces of glass shattered on the floor. My hands trembled as I paced back and forth. Excuses for breaking Mom's favorite vase zipped through my head. I could feel tears rising in my eyes. My head felt hot and dizzy. I was going to be in big trouble.

Read about a mistake I made.

Writer's Checklist

✓ Does the writer include interesting words; details about size, shape, color; or other features?

✓ Does the writer describe how the moment felt and sounded?

☑ Does Drew **show** you the moment as though you were seeing it through her eyes?

Talk About It

How would you describe your neighborhood or community? How has it changed over time?

LOG ON ▶ Find out more about communities at **www.macmillanmh.com**.

Communities

Vocabulary

- culture
- communities
- immigrants
- established
- traditional

Mesa Verde National Park in Colorado is home to 600 Anasazi cliff dwellings. At one time, thousands of Anasazi lived there.

Living in the Cliffs

The Anasazi are among the first peoples to live in the American Southwest. The history and the **culture** of these ancient peoples are not completely known.

Historians know that around A.D. 1, the mysterious Anasazi, also known as Ancient Pueblo People, arrived in the Southwest. At first, there was plenty of food and water for them to survive. But when the weather got hotter and drier, there was a scarcity of food and land for growing. The Anasazi had to move.

As time passed, the Anasazi moved from underground houses to above-ground dwellings. Many made homes on the sides of cliffs. The cliff houses were safe from enemies and the weather.

Around A.D. 1300 the Anasazi left their homes in the Southwest. No one knows for sure why they left or where they went. Some scientists think the dry weather forced them to leave.

Luckily, many Anasazi homes still exist. These ancient **communities** give us clues about life for the Ancient Puebloans.

Clues in a Cave

Archaeologists are studying ancient objects in a rock shelter called Daisy Cave. The site is on San Miguel Island, near the California coast. Scientists think people began living in the cave at least 12,000 years ago!

Thousands of years ago, North America was settled by **immigrants** from Asia who traveled down the west coast of North America. What kind of people lived in Daisy Cave? Why did they come here? The scientists hope to find the answers.

San Miguel Island

Old Town News

The streets of Old Town, in San Diego, have a story to tell. Old Town is a community known as the birthplace of California.

People called Kumevaay lived in Old Town about 9,000 years ago. Then in 1769 European settlers **established** the first Spanish neighborhood.

During the 1800s, Old Town was the site of many California firsts. The state's first newspaper office opened there in 1851. The first schoolhouse in Southern California was built in Old Town in 1865.

The Immaculate Conception Church in Old Town opened to the public in 1917.

Today, Old Town brings the past to life celebrating Latino culture and history. **Traditional** Mexican foods and crafts are featured for the annual Cinco de Mayo fiesta. Old Town's streets come alive with the sights and sounds of its early residents.

LOG ON ▶ Find out more about ancient communities at **www.macmillanmh.com**.

CA **Comprehension**

Genre

Nonfiction A nonfiction article gives information about real people, places, or things.

Monitor Comprehension

✓ Main Idea and Details
A main idea is the purpose of the article. Details support the main idea.

Coasting to California

How did Chinese immigrants succeed despite hard times?

For much of its history, California has attracted Chinese **immigrants**. Life was often hard for these newcomers. But thanks to their skills and hard work, Chinese immigrants made their mark here.

The discovery of gold in 1848 sparked a large wave of immigration. Nearly 500,000 people from around the world rushed to California with dreams of becoming rich. Among the people looking for gold were people from China. By 1851 there were 25,000 Chinese people living in California.

Chinese immigrants came to the United States to seek a better life.

Keeping Their Culture

Chinese immigrants usually came through the port of San Francisco. They formed **communities** in many California cities. In each city they tried to hold onto their **culture**. Chinese immigrants settled in neighborhoods known as Chinatowns.

One of the first Chinatowns was **established** in a Sacramento neighborhood in 1869. Here, Chinese stores and restaurants lined the streets. Many people in these Chinatowns knew each other from back home in China.

Working for a Living

As California grew, new jobs were created. Thousands more immigrants from all over the world came for work. The Chinese weren't allowed to start their own businesses except in the Chinatowns. Many immigrants became servants. Others were hired as waiters, miners, or laundry workers.

The Central Pacific Railroad was one company that hired Chinese workers. They helped build railroad tracks. The workers blasted mountains. They dug tunnels. They fixed roads. This work was dangerous and did not pay well.

Neighborhoods where many Chinese immigrants settled became Chinatowns.

The Chinese tried hard to make a living. Some used their farming skills. Others were good at fishing. Chinese fishers formed communities in Monterey, San Diego, San Francisco, and San Luis Obispo. They built **traditional** boats to fish for shrimp.

Chinatowns Then

In 1882 an anti-immigration law passed which stopped Chinese immigration. Other laws said Chinese immigrants couldn't be United States citizens. Life became even harder for Chinese Americans. Most had to live in Chinatowns in large cities. These Chinatowns had become poor and unsafe.

Conditions changed in 1943 when the anti-immigration law was abolished. Now more Chinese arrived in the United States in search of a better life.

Chinese fishers lived in villages called shrimp camps.

Visitors to Los Angeles's Chinatown pass through the decorative Dragon's Gate.

Chinatowns Now

San Francisco's Chinatown is a popular tourist spot. More people visit this area than the Golden Gate Bridge. Pass under the huge Dragon's Gate to enter Chinatown and walk through crowded streets of stores selling Chinese clothes and art. Food markets display unusual products used in Chinese cooking. There is even a fortune cookie factory that makes 20,000 cookies a day!

Another California Chinatown is in Los Angeles. This new Chinatown was rebuilt in the 1930s to look like a city in China, with colorful buildings and curved roofs. Its pedestrian mall, shops, and restaurants bring many tourists. It's a star attraction!

CA Critical Thinking

1. According to the **details** of this article, what were some of the hardships faced by the Chinese immigrants?

2. What are some characteristics of a Chinatown?

3. What different cultural areas are found in your community?

4. What are some ways in which people keep their traditional culture alive, according to this article and "Old Town News"?

217

A Treat of a Street

Traditional artists and vendors sell Mexican-style products on Olvera Street.

Each year two million tourists visit Olvera Street, a famous street in Los Angeles, California. People come to see its colorful outdoor market, to eat at its traditional Mexican and Latin American restaurants, and to learn about California history.

Olvera Street is known as the birthplace of Los Angeles. Historic buildings remain to show us its past. Avila Adobe, the oldest house in Los Angeles, is on this historic street. The adobe was built in 1818.

Olvera Street has changed several times over the centuries. In the 1880s, as Los Angeles began to grow, a power station was built here. The station helped power electric streetcars. As Los Angeles grew, Olvera Street became more rundown.

In 1926 a woman named Christine Sterling raised money to improve and restore Olvera Street. Mexican restaurants opened up. Musicians and dancers performed in the streets. Olvera Street has gone from being the birthplace of a city to a rundown alley to a historic marketplace. It has many stories to tell us.

Go on

 CA Standards Practice

Directions: Now answer Numbers 1–5. Base your answers on the article "A Treat of a Street."

1. **This article is MOSTLY about**

   A   Olvera Street today.

   B   the history of Avila Adobe.

   C   the history of Olvera Street.

   D   Olvera Street's beginning.

Tip

Think about the entire passage to choose the best answer.

2. **Around 1926 Olvera Street was**

   A   a bustling city neighborhood.

   B   a badly neglected, rundown area.

   C   the home of the city's mayor.

   D   the most famous street in Los Angeles.

3. **How does Olvera Street help Los Angeles?**

   A   It is an important tourist attraction.

   B   It gives jobs to musicians and dancers.

   C   It shows a typical, modern Los Angeles to tourists.

   D   It contains Los Angeles's only outdoor market.

4. **Describe a visit you and your family make to Olvera Street. Use DETAILS from the article as well as your imagination in your answer.**

5. **Do you think it was important to save Olvera Street? Use DETAILS from the article to support your answer.**

Write on Demand

CA Many people are afraid of things like the dark or snakes.

Think of something you are afraid of and the reasons why.

Now <u>write about</u> what you are afraid of and <u>explain why</u>.

Expository writing explains, defines, or tells how to do something.

To figure out if a writing prompt asks for expository writing, look for clue words, such as <u>explain why</u> or <u>write about</u>.

Below, see how one student begins a response to the prompt above.

The events explain why the writer is afraid of spiders.

I am very frightened of spiders. Big, small, brown, and black—they all make me want to scream and run away quickly.

It all started when I was three. My favorite coat was green with yellow snaps. My mom handed me my coat to put on by myself. I felt so grown-up because I had just learned how to fasten the snaps. Suddenly, as I was snapping the last snap, I looked down and saw a huge daddy longlegs spider crawling across my sleeve! I tore off the coat immediately and started yelling and running around.

That is not the only reason I am afraid of spiders.

Writing Prompt

Respond in writing to the prompt below. Write for 8 minutes. Write as much as you can, as well as you can. Review the hints below before and after you write.

CA

Communities are full of good citizens.

Think about what being a good citizen means to you.

Now write about what being a good citizen means to you.

Writing Hints for Prompts

- ☑ Read the prompt carefully.
- ☑ Plan your writing by organizing your ideas.
- ☑ Support your ideas by telling more about each reason.
- ☑ Use complete sentences.
- ☑ Choose descriptive words that show what you mean.
- ☑ Review and edit your writing.

WORKING TOGETHER

CA **Talk About It**

What are some ways that you can work with others to help your school or community?

LOG ON ▶ Find out more about working together at **www.macmillanmh.com**.

GORILLA GARDEN

by Michael Feldman

Have you ever taken a **tour** of a zoo? If so, it's likely that the person who led you through the zoo helped you to learn a lot about the animals.

Amelia Rinas is a high school student who lives in Ohio. One day Amelia visited the Cleveland Metroparks Zoo. She worried about the gorillas she saw there. She wondered if they were getting the right foods.

Amelia read all she could about gorillas and learned what they like to eat. Then she started a "gorilla garden." She grows the fruits and vegetables that gorillas love to eat. Some of those foods are tomatoes, carrots, and strawberries. Amelia works with other **volunteers** in her community who use their extra time to help Amelia and the gorillas. When they take the food to the zoo, the gorillas are **thrilled**. They look so excited!

Who is responsible for Amelia's interest in animals? Amelia is a member of Roots & Shoots. Its members are young people who care about animals and the environment. They helped Amelia understand that animals need our care, too. The **slogan** on the Roots & Shoots Web site is "Inspire, take action, make a difference." These words tell what the group is all about. The group urges kids and grownups, including parents and teachers, to do what they can to make a difference where they live.

Amelia believes that both people and animals **deserve** to be treated well.

When interviewed about her project, Amelia said, "I joined Roots & Shoots because I wanted to make a difference in the world."

There are many ways to make a difference in the world. Amelia Rinas's gorilla garden has helped make gorillas happier and healthier.

Reread for Comprehension

Monitor Comprehension

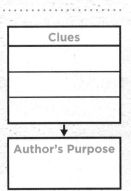

Author's Purpose An author writes to entertain, inform, or persuade. Usually, an author will give readers clues that help readers figure out the **author's purpose**. You can help monitor your understanding of an article by thinking about the author's purpose. Reread the article. Use your Author's Purpose Chart to record clues to help you figure out why the author wrote this article.

Clues

↓

Author's Purpose

(CA) Comprehension

Genre

Nonfiction Some nonfiction articles give information about real people, places, or things.

Monitor Comprehension

Author's Purpose

As you read, use your Author's Purpose Map.

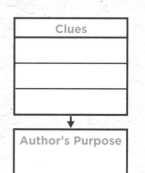

Clues

↓

Author's Purpose

Read to Find Out

Why did the author write about Angel?

Here's My Dollar

By Gary Soto

Angel poses with her cat.

How tall is a hero? If you had ever met nine-year-old Angel Arellano, you'd know a hero is four feet two inches tall. Angel's story began on Thanksgiving Day. She was in the kitchen listening to her Great-Grandmother Sandy.

"The zoo has money problems," Great-Grandmother Sandy remarked.

Angel listened. She heard that Fresno's Chaffee Zoo didn't have enough money to take care of its animals. Angel wondered what would happen to the elephants, the hippo, and her favorite reptile, the boa constrictor.

Angel loved animals. She planned to study them and become a zoologist when she grew up. In their own apartment in Fresno, Angel's family had four cats—Buster, Krystal, Rex, and Oreo. Angel took good care of them and made sure that they always had food and water.

> **Author's Purpose**
> Why does the author tell us about Angel's pets?

Angel holds a skink at the Chaffee Zoo.

Angel felt sorry for the zoo animals. While the grownups were cooking Thanksgiving dinner, Angel was cooking up a way to help the animals. She decided to write a letter to show how she felt.

When she finished writing, Angel showed the letter to her mom and her aunt. They changed some of the words and fixed the spelling. Then Angel copied her letter onto fancy stationery and added a **slogan** at the bottom: "Give a dollar, save a life." She slipped a dollar into the envelope and addressed it to *The Fresno Bee*, the local newspaper.

Angel's letter to The Fresno Bee

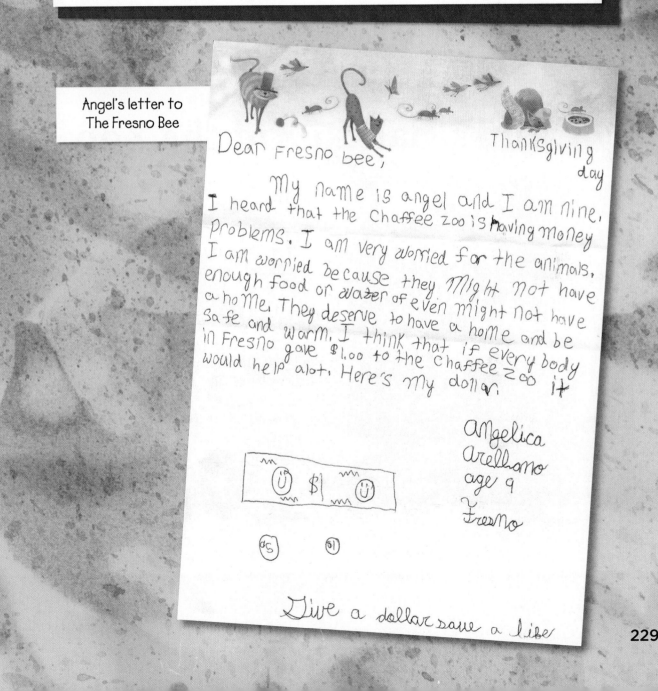

Dear Fresno bee,

Thanksgiving day

My name is angel and I am nine. I heard that the Chaffee zoo is having money problems. I am very worried for the animals. I am worried because they might not have enough food or water or even might not have a home. They deserve to have a home and be safe and warm. I think that if everybody in Fresno gave $1.00 to the Chaffee zoo it would help alot. Here's my dollar.

Angelica Arellano age 9 Fresno

Give a dollar save a life

Angel hoped that other people might send a dollar, too, after they had read her letter. She didn't know that the zoo needed three million dollars, but that wouldn't have stopped her anyhow. Angel was a girl on a mission!

A week later, a man from *The Fresno Bee* came to take a picture of Angel. A few days after that, Angel's letter was published in *The Fresno Bee*. Almost immediately, people began sending in checks and dollar bills. Angel's letter was working!

Child's Call to Aid the Zoo

Angel Arellano collects money for the Chaffee Zoo.

By Jim Davis

Nine-year-old Angel Arellano is sparking a grass-roots effort to help the Chaffee Zoo through its financial plight. The little girl sent a letter to *The Bee* and enclosed a $1 donation for the zoo. She asked others to donate as well. "I just hope it will help," Angel said. "I want the animals to be safe and warm and let them get fed like my letter said." Dozens have followed Angel's lead, sending donations ranging from $1 to a $1,000 check that arrived Thursday. After just two days' mail, the zoo has received $5,084.

Text from an article about Angel in *The Fresno Bee*, December 6, 2003

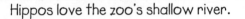

Hippos love the zoo's shallow river.

At school, Angel went to each classroom to read the letter that appeared in the newspaper. She asked her schoolmates to give money to the zoo. An empty water jug was placed in each classroom and in the main office. Students—and parents—began to fill the jugs with coins and dollar bills.

Angel's letter had touched the community of Fresno—and beyond. Donations for the Chaffee Zoo began to arrive from all over California. One donation came from as far away as England. It seemed as if the whole world wanted to help the zoo.

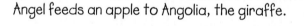

Angel feeds an apple to Angolia, the giraffe.

The people at the Chaffee Zoo were **thrilled**. They invited Angel and her family to the zoo. They wanted to thank Angel in person and give her a private **tour**.

At the zoo, Angel fed grapes to the chimpanzees. She fed the hippo and the buffalo, too. In a daring mood, Angel placed a slice of apple in her mouth. She stretched her neck toward Angolia, the giraffe, who leaned its long neck down and swiped the apple from her mouth!

Angel went on being a regular kid—for a while. Before long, she was asked to make public appearances to talk about the zoo. The zoo still needed money, and Angel was happy to help. The principal of her school drove her to other schools in the area. He was just as concerned about the zoo animals as Angel.

"The zoo needs your help," Angel told the other children. "We can all make a difference."

During these appearances, Angel autographed pieces of paper, posters, and lots of shirts and caps. When reporters interviewed her, she tried to be herself. She spoke from her heart.

Angel prepares to make a public service announcement.

233

Next, Angel was asked to appear on television. She was invited to be on a popular talk show. Angel flew from Fresno to Los Angeles. It was the first time she was ever on a plane!

At the television studio, Angel entered the stage to applause and her favorite rock music. She smiled and waved. The audience was rooting for her. They were rooting for the zoo animals back in Fresno, too.

More donations arrived after Angel's appearance on television. The Chaffee Zoo got larger and larger checks. One was for $10,000. Another was for $15,000. And one was for $50,000!

Of course, many donations were still just for one dollar. Children were sending in what they had, just as Angel had done on Thanksgiving Day.

Angel boards a plane to make a television appearance.

Zookeeper Mary helps Angel hold a boa constrictor.

Everyone was behind Angel and the zoo. High school teams held car washes to raise money. **Volunteers** showed up at the zoo to help paint and clean up. A local business made T-shirts with a picture of the zoo on the front.

The zookeepers were very happy. Ray Navarro is the person most responsible for the animals. He has hauled thousands of buckets of water for the animals. He has pushed wheelbarrows of hay for the elephants, the giraffes, and the zebras. "Angel opened the eyes of Fresno," said Ray. "She made us see that people can make a difference."

Author's Purpose
Why did the author choose to write about Angel?

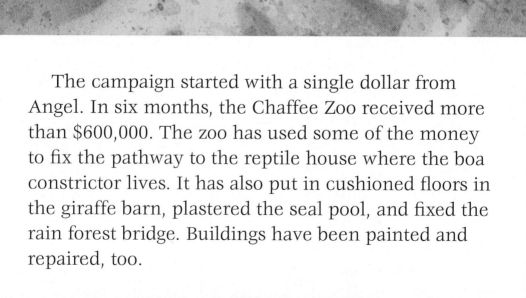

Angel's fundraising efforts are displayed on a billboard at the zoo.

The campaign started with a single dollar from Angel. In six months, the Chaffee Zoo received more than $600,000. The zoo has used some of the money to fix the pathway to the reptile house where the boa constrictor lives. It has also put in cushioned floors in the giraffe barn, plastered the seal pool, and fixed the rain forest bridge. Buildings have been painted and repaired, too.

The campaign to save the Chaffee Zoo has been exciting. People from Fresno are proud that a young girl woke up their own community spirit. The zoo is looking better and better. And even though the zoo animals can't speak human languages, if they could, they might say, "You are a hero to us, Angel Arellano. You **deserve** our thanks for saving our zoo."

The zoo's seals enjoy a swim in a newly plastered pool, thanks to Angel.

Here's Our Author

Gary Soto was born and raised in Fresno, California, which is also the hometown of the Chaffee Zoo. He has written many poems and stories for children and adults. In his spare time, Gary loves to read, play tennis and basketball, and travel. He still visits Fresno often, and there is a library named for him at Winchell Elementary School in Fresno.

Other books by Gary Soto: *Baseball in April* and *Chato's Kitchen*

 LOG ON ▶ Find out more about Gary Soto at **www.macmillanmh.com**.

CA Author's Purpose

Suppose you were the author of *Here's My Dollar.* Describe why you wrote this article and how you achieved your goal. Use details from the article in your answer.

CA Critical Thinking

Summarize

Summarize *Here's My Dollar.* Use your Author's Purpose Chart to help you.

Clues

↓

Author's Purpose

Think and Compare

1. Why do you think Gary Soto wrote *Here's My Dollar*? Use examples and information from the article to tell the **author's purpose**. Monitor Comprehension: Author's Purpose

2. Reread pages 229–231. Explain how Angel "touched the community" of Fresno and beyond. How did *The Fresno Bee* help do this? Use article details in your answer. **Analyze**

3. Think of a good cause in your own community that needs help, such as a school, library, or park. How would you encourage people to help? **Apply**

4. Why is using a **slogan** a good way to help raise money for a cause? Use information from the story to support your ideas. **Synthesize**

5. Reread "Gorilla Garden" on pages 224–225. How are Amelia and Angel alike? Describe the different ways they help animals. **Reading/ Writing Across Texts**

Poetry

Poetry uses rhyme, rhythm, and repetition to express feelings and ideas.

Literary Elements

A **Rhyme Scheme** is the pattern of rhymes in the last words of lines.

Repetition happens when words or phrases are repeated in a poem. A line that is repeated throughout is called a **refrain**.

The last line of each stanza is the refrain.

Neighbors

When I had the sniffles,
Your mom sent me stew.
You needed a project.
My daddy helped you.
Your dad helps us paint from ceiling to floor.
Neighbors are friends who live just next door.

I call you up
When I know you feel down.
When Fluffy was lost,
We looked all over town.
It's my turn to rake when your arms get
   too sore.
Neighbors are friends who live just next door.

—Mari Paz Pradillo

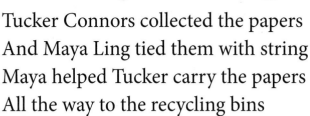

Recycling

Tucker Connors collected the papers
And Maya Ling tied them with string
Maya helped Tucker carry the papers
All the way to the recycling bins

Won Tan collected the cans
And Ruby Dean washed them all clean
Ruby helped Won carry the cans
All the way to the recycling bins

When we recycle, we help the plants
We help the creatures, from eagles to ants
We help make the world a healthier place
For one and for all in the human race

—J. Z. Belle

Plants and *ants* rhyme, as do *place* and *race*. The rhyme scheme for this stanza is **AA BB**.

CA Critical Thinking

1. What are some repetitions in "Recycling"? **Repetition**

2. What does the poet want to tell you about neighbors? **Analyze**

3. Compare these two poems about helping and *Here's My Dollar.* How are these selections alike? How are they different? **Reading/Writing Across Texts**

LOG ON ▶ Find out more about poetry at www.macmillanmh.com.

✔ **Strong Verbs**

Include **strong verbs** that tell about the moment you are writing about.

Reading and Writing Connection

Read the passage below. Notice how author Gary Soto uses strong verbs in his article.

An excerpt from
Here's My Dollar

The author uses strong verbs to help us imagine exactly how people in the article moved. The author picks out verbs that put clear pictures in our head.

She stretched her neck toward Angolia, the giraffe, who leaned its long neck down and swiped the apple from her mouth....

[Ray Navarro] has hauled thousands of buckets of water for the animals. He has pushed wheelbarrows of hay for the elephants, the giraffes, and the zebras.

Here's My Dollar
By Gary Soto

Read and Find

Read Aldo's writing below. How does he use strong verbs to help you imagine the moment? Use the tips below to help you.

Our New Trampoline
by Aldo S.

As soon as *my dad finished building our new trampoline, my sister and I scrambled up onto it.* It is kind of high, so *we had to grip the sides to help drag ourselves onto it. Then we started bouncing!* At first *we just jumped up and down, but soon we twisted and tumbled as we tried new tricks.*

Read about our new trampoline.

Writer's Checklist

✓ Does the writer choose verbs that describe specific actions?

✓ Does the writer use several different verbs instead of the same verb over and over?

☑ Do the verbs **show** you what is happening? Is there a picture in your mind?

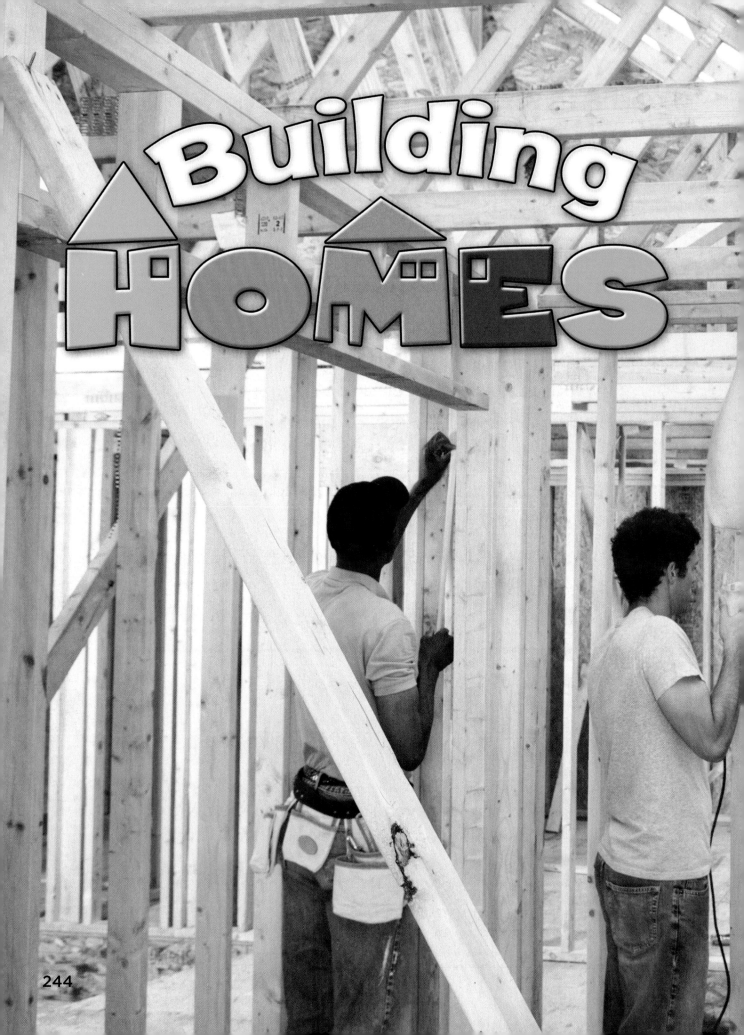

Building HOMES

CA Talk About It

How are these people helping others? What types of work are they doing?

LOG ON ▶ Find out more about building homes at www.macmillanmh.com.

245

What Should I Be?

by Carol R.

All around my neighborhood, I see people working to protect and help me and my family. Firefighters, letter carriers, and police officers are community workers. They make my neighborhood a better place to live. When I am older, I would like to be a community worker, but which job should I choose?

Letter Carriers

Letter carriers deliver our mail and drop off packages. They work in every town and city in the United States.

The letter carrier in my neighborhood is Mr. Vasquez. He works downtown, walking from block to block to deliver mail to each address along the route. He doesn't carry big boxes, like the ones that hold stoves and washing machines. Trucks deliver **appliances** like those! Maybe I will be a letter carrier.

Police Officers

Police officers, like Officer Morena, keep us safe. Home and business **owners** depend on the police to guard our families, our property, and our streets.

Police may also work at sites where the **construction** of new buildings takes place. They help keep the **project** running smoothly. Officer Morena can find lost people and help if there is an accident. Her special **equipment**, such as a two-way radio, allows her to talk to other officers. Being a police officer might be a good job.

Firefighters

Firefighters are brave, like Chief Cole. They risk their lives to save people caught in fires. They also check smoke alarms in schools, as well as fire hydrants along the road to make sure they are tightly sealed. **Leaky** hydrants may not have enough water when the time comes to fight a fire.

Chief Cole is a good firefighter. Maybe I will be one too, someday.

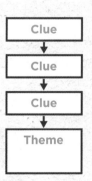

Reread for **Comprehension**

Analyze Story Structure

Theme A **theme** is the message an author wants to present in a story or article. An article's theme is usually not stated. To find the theme, analyze the story structure for **clues**. Think about the characters' words and actions and how the story begins and ends.

Reread the selection. Use your Theme Map to record clues that help you figure out the article's theme.

Clue
↓
Clue
↓
Clue
↓
Theme

CA Comprehension

Genre

Fiction is an invented story that could have happened in real life.

Analyze Story Structure

✔ Theme

As you read, use your Theme Map.

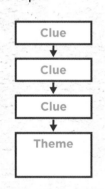

Clue
↓
Clue
↓
Clue
↓
Theme

Read to Find Out

What is the theme of this story?

A Castle on Viola Street

by DyAnne DiSalvo

Award Winning Author

In the old days, before I was ten, we rented an apartment on Emerald Street. It was a small place to live in for one whole family, but somehow we made the room.

There always seemed to be enough to go around, even with five people at our table.

Every morning my father would get up even before the sun. "Someday things will change around here," he would whisper to me. He usually said this during the winter when the house was beginning to feel chilly. Then he'd kiss us good-bye, tuck up our blankets, and leave for his job at the diner.

My mother worked part-time in the downtown bakery while my sisters and I were at school. After school she'd sit on the stoop and watch us play.

Sometimes my mother would flip through a magazine. She'd show me pictures of houses with gardens and porches. They all looked like castles to me. I'd puff out my cheeks when I looked at our place. It was old and peeling and sorry.

That's when my mother would hug me and say, "Our family is rich in more ways than we can count."

> **Theme**
> Why does the mother look at pictures of houses?

On Saturday mornings my mother would weigh my pockets down with quarters for the Laundromat.

"Hold Andy's hand," she'd tell my sister.

Then my mother would slip two brown-bagged lunches in the wagon with a dollar for a treat. My sister and I would bump our cart to the Soap & Go on Viola Street.

Now, across the street from the Soap & Go were three boarded-up houses. My father said it was a shame. "Somebody should do something about that," he'd say whenever he saw them. So when a truck pulled up and workers unloaded **equipment**, I started to pay attention.

"What's going on over there?" a lady at the Soap &
Go asked.

Mr. Rivera pointed to a flier that was posted up front.

"I'll bet it has something to do with this," he told
her. The flier had a picture of a house and said
YOU TOO CAN OWN A HOME.

After our laundry was dried and folded, I took my sister by
the hand and rushed our wagon back to Emerald Street.

At supper I told my parents all about what I had heard and seen. My father scrambled eggs with extra zest, and my mother put ice in our water.

"There's a meeting tonight," I said. "Seven o'clock at the school."

Later on, when my parents came home, they were just as excited as I was.

"This organization buys empty houses and fixes them up like new!" said my mother.

"And if you're interested in helping to fix up a house for other people," my father continued, "then one day other people will help fix up a house for you."

That sounded like a good plan to me. It would be nice to live in a house that wasn't so chilly in winter.

"So we signed up," my father told me. "Can we count on you to help?"

I hugged them so tight I almost fell out of bed. I think they knew my answer.

Well, you know how sometimes, when you never believe that anything will ever be different, then one morning you just wake up and nothing is the same? That's what happened to our family that spring when the **project** on Viola Street began.

Clang! Bang! Bang! Smash! Those workers started early.

"Take a good look," my mother told us. "That's what we'll be doing soon."

"Are all those people getting a house?" I asked.

"Some of them will," my mother said. "But anyone who wants to can help. It's called volunteering."

Piece by piece, the inside of the first house came apart—one old bathtub, some cabinets, sinks. Slats of wood and piping piled up like a mountain full of junk in the Dumpster.

Most people on the block were happy about the project, but other people were not. The lady next door said, "No banging before nine o'clock!" Some people laughed and said out loud, "Who would want a house in a neighborhood like this?"

But my father would smile and whisper to me, "Sometimes new things are hard to get used to and people are slow to change."

On the weekends, when our family showed up, a leader called out the assignments.

"Everyone here will have a special job to do," she said.

My mother scraped wallpaper off crusty walls that
crumbled like toast. My father and I worked together.
He lifted up old linoleum tiles by sliding a cat-hammer
underneath. My job was to carefully hammer down nails on
the floorboards when he was through.

Some volunteers, like us, hoped to have a house
one day.

"We're looking forward to living in a place without
broken windows and **leaky** pipes," Mr. and Mrs. Rivera said.

My father said he couldn't wait to have a house that
would have heat all winter.

My sisters were still too young to help with all the **construction**. But my mother told them, "Being little is no excuse not to pitch in." She had them squeeze juice from bags of lemons to make fresh lemonade. Then they took turns pouring and passing the cups all around.

At the end of the day there was always a lot of sweeping to do.

"I've never seen so much dust in my life," Mrs. Tran said, covering her nose.

My mother held a dustpan while I pushed the broom. My sisters giggled whenever they saw me wearing my safety mask.

> **Theme**
> Why is the family working so hard?

262

On Saturday nights I'd be so tired, I'd practically fall asleep right after supper.

"You're doing good work," my father would say. And he'd thank me for helping our family. He'd say, "Big dreams are built little by little, and we are making a start."

In those four months I learned a lot about putting things together. Once I even found a piece of wood that my father said I could keep. I thought that maybe I could use it to make something on my own.

One day Mr. Tran gave everyone some news. The new house would be theirs!

"Everything is beautiful," Mrs. Tran said. She stood smiling inside the framed front door. She watched her daughter paint the big front room. The kitchen had shiny linoleum floors and brand-new **appliances**. There even was a washing machine! Upstairs was a bathroom and three carpeted bedrooms. Out back there was a place for a garden.

When the Tran family moved in, they threw a potluck supper. My father and I took care to make something extra special that night.

"Since I've been promoted to cook, I like to whip up a storm," he said.

We not only celebrated the Tran family's being the **owners** of their new home, but we also celebrated because we knew we were one house closer to our dream.

Things were really changing on Viola Street now. "This neighborhood looks like it's shaping up," the lady at the Soap & Go said. Volunteers were working on two more empty houses. And of course the Trans next door didn't mind when we wanted to get to work early.

This fall our family was notified that we'd be working on our own house next spring—number one-forty-six Viola Street. Whenever we pass it, my mother says, "I can imagine it finished already." I've already got my bedroom picked out. It's the one with the window by the yard.

During the winter, I made a birdhouse from my piece of wood and gave it to my mother. My mother was more than pleased about that. She said, thanks to me, now even the birds would have a nice little place to call home.

I used to dream that we had a million dollars to buy a house of our own. But in real life all it cost us was a lot of hard work. Anyway, it seems to me like all the money in the world couldn't buy us what we have now on Viola Street. It's just as my father says: Big dreams are built little by little, and we have made a start.

The Nuts and Bolts on DyAnne

Author and Illustrator

DyAnne DiSalvo says that before she starts a book, she can see the whole thing in her mind. Then she gets to work. Sometimes she does research and takes pictures. Other times she just draws a picture she has in her head. DyAnne often uses things she's done to write her books. Just like the characters in this story, DyAnne joined a special group that builds houses for people. She says that her stories are a little bit fiction and a little bit nonfiction.

Other books by DyAnne DiSalvo:
City Green and *A Dog Like Jack*

A DOG LIKE JACK

City Green
DyAnne DiSalvo-Ryan

LOG ON ▶ Find out more about DyAnne DiSalvo at **www.macmillanmh.com**.

CA Author's Purpose

What was the author's purpose for writing *A Castle on Viola Street*? Did DyAnne DiSalvo want to entertain or inform readers? How do you know?

Critical Thinking

Summarize

Use the Theme Map to help you summarize
A Castle on Viola Street. Tell about the setting,
the characters, and the events.

Clue
↓
Clue
↓
Clue
↓
Theme

Think and Compare

1. Use your Theme Map to identify the **theme** of *A Castle on Viola Street.* What story details tell about the theme?
Analyze Story Structure: Theme

2. Reread page 251 of *A Castle on Viola Street.* What does the mother mean when she says that the family is "rich"? Use story details in your answer. **Evaluate**

3. Which **appliances** in your home are most important to you? Explain. **Apply**

4. What can a family learn from helping another family build a home? **Evaluate**

5. Read pages 246–247. How are the community workers in "What Should I Be?" like the characters in *A Castle on Viola Street*? **Reading/Writing Across Texts**

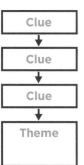

HOMES
for Families

by Angel Gracia

Everyone needs a home, but finding one can be difficult. The cost of buying a home is often very high, and so is the cost to **rent** a place to live by the month.

One Solution to the Problem

A group called Habitat for Humanity helps provide homes for **needy** families. Habitat for Humanity's work is true to its name: Habitat means "homes," and humanity means "people." This **organization** works with families to help them build comfortable, low-cost homes of their own.

How Habitat for Humanity Works

Habitat for Humanity is made up mostly of **volunteers** who work for free because they like to help other people.

Families who need homes can contact the group. The group then chooses deserving families and helps them build a home. Before the families get help building their own homes, they must help build homes for other families.

Volunteers work on a Habitat for Humanity home in LaGrange, Georgia.

The hard work of many people is needed to build a home.

Former President Jimmy Carter helps build a Habitat for Humanity home.

All Over the World

Habitat for Humanity builds homes in many places besides the United States. Their work can also be seen in other countries such as Thailand, South Africa, and Guatemala. In each country, the houses are built from materials that are available nearby. That makes it easier for families to keep their homes in good shape and for the homes to look as if they fit into the neighborhood.

Features in a Textbook

Using Features in a Textbook

The following textbook features are used in this article to help you understand what you are reading.

- An **Introduction** is a brief explanation of the text.
- A **Heading** appears before a piece of writing.
- **Boldface Type** calls attention to important words.
- **Different-sized Type** shows a heading or important words.
- A **Caption** explains the photo.

 ## Critical Thinking

1. Read the caption for the photo on page 271. Where was the photo taken? **Using Features in a Textbook**

2. Suppose that you and your family are working with Habitat for Humanity. What jobs do you think you could or would like to do? **Synthesize**

3. Think about this article and *A Castle on Viola Street.* Compare Habitat for Humanity with the organization that Andy and his family volunteered for. How are they similar? **Reading/Writing Across Texts**

 ### History/Social Science Activity

Ask your family members and friends what kinds of volunteer work they do or know about. Use your research to write a paragraph about one interesting volunteer job.

 Find out more about volunteering at **www.macmillanmh.com**.

Writing

CA

✓ Strong Verbs

Use **strong verbs** to help your reader see exactly what you are describing in your writing.

Read the passage below. Notice how author DyAnne DiSalvo uses strong verbs in her story.

An excerpt from
A Castle on Viola Street

The author uses strong verbs to help us imagine exactly how each member of the family helped out. The author picks out verbs that show how the characters moved and worked.

My mother scraped wallpaper off crusty walls that crumbled like toast. My father and I worked together. He lifted up old linoleum tiles by sliding a cat-hammer underneath. My job was to carefully hammer down nails on the floorboards when he was through.

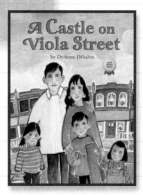

A Castle on Viola Street
by DyAnne DiSalvo

Read and Find

Read Lenny's writing below. How does he use strong verbs to help you imagine the moment? Use the tips below to help you.

Jiggle Jiggle Jell-O

by Lenny S.

My mom plopped a big scoop of pink Jell-O into my dish. I examined this odd-looking dessert. I poked the blob with my spoon, and it began to wiggle and jiggle. As it shivered in the bowl, my spoon slid smoothly into it. Gulp!

Read about a cool dessert.

Writer's Checklist

✓ Does the writer choose **strong verbs** that describe specific actions?

✓ Does the writer use several different verbs instead of the same verb over and over?

☑ Is there a verb in this piece that makes you think of a sound or a feeling?

Nancy's Library

✔ **Review**

Main Idea and Details
Character, Setting, Plot
Theme
Multiple-Meaning Words
Features of a Textbook

Nancy was upset. She used to love going to the library across the street. Now nobody wanted to go there anymore. The building needed to be repainted. The lawn and sidewalk out front were full of garbage.

What could she do? Nancy's mother encouraged her to think about how they could help. "Try making a list," suggested her mother.

Nancy took a long time writing all of her ideas. Her mother came in to check on her.

"Well," Nancy said, "we could call the town offices to see if they could help us clean the trash. We could see if they have people who paint. What do you think, Mom?"

"I think those are great ideas!" said Nancy's mother. When they contacted the town office, they learned that the money for libraries had been cut. The people at the town park offices suggested that Nancy organize a neighborhood cleanup.

Nancy's mother promised to help her plan the cleanup.

"Okay," Nancy said, "let's make a list of what we'll need."

"First," Nancy's mother replied, "we'll need lots of big trash bags for trash."

Nancy added, "And paint. Plus we have to choose a date for the cleanup and make signs to get people to come."

Soon the big day arrived. Nancy had contacted all of her friends, and they were there at the library. Some of their parents were there, too. Within a couple of hours, six trash bags were filled. The grass was almost clean! Some parents repainted the door, walls, and railings. The whole area looked much better. Nancy felt proud.

"But how will we keep it this way?" Nancy asked her mother.

"Why not ask everybody else for ideas this time," suggested her mother.

Nancy asked her friends and their families. She was amazed at what they had to say. Nearly all of them said that they would come again to do another cleanup. "We need this library," said one dad. "You kids should have a safe, clean place to read and study."

"Plus, the lawn is a great place for story hour," said one of the moms. "Let's try to keep it nice."

"Thank you so much!" cried Nancy.

"No, thank *you*," said Nancy's mother. "You're the one who got us moving and gave us back our library!"

A Change in PLANS

The playground at Wilson School has been around for many years. It was just the right size when the school was built. Now the school has many more students, so the playground just isn't big enough.

In October of last year, the Smithville City Council promised to build a bigger playground this summer. The new playground will have more swings, slides, and basketball hoops, as well as a modern jungle gym.

On Monday night, the Wilson School Parents Group learned that the playground will not be finished this summer. John Tang, the Smithville City Council President, spoke to the parents. He said that work will start this summer, but it will take a year for the playground to be built. In the meantime, students will have no playground.

Many parents were upset. They said that students, parents, and school staff have been looking forward to the new playground for a long time.

Why the Plan Changed

During the meeting one parent spoke up. "Why will it take a whole year to build the playground?" she asked.

Mr. Tang said that construction workers will tear up the old playground during the summer. Then throughout the year, they will work on the playground. Mr. Tang explained that the construction workers are also working on many other projects.

Parents Propose a Solution

The Wilson School Parents Group met again on Tuesday night to talk about the problem. After a few hours, they came up with a solution.

Parents asked the city council to wait until the fall to begin the project. Builders could do the work during the school year. In the meantime, the old playground would still be there for students to use this summer. In addition, parents volunteered to donate their time during the year to keep the project on schedule.

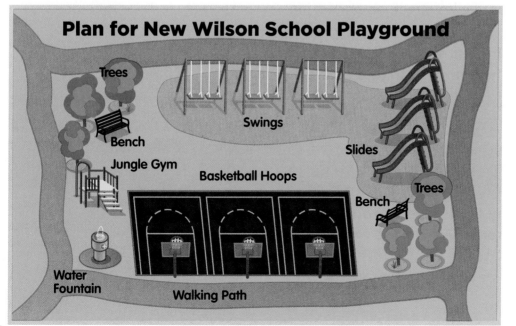

Plan for New Wilson School Playground

Trees

Swings

Bench

Slides

Jungle Gym

Basketball Hoops

Trees

Bench

Water Fountain

Walking Path

CA Critical Thinking

Now answer numbers 1 through 4. Base your answers on the passage "Nancy's Library."

1. Why is Nancy unhappy at the BEGINNING of the passage?

A   Nancy thought no one would help her.

B   Nancy was upset that the library was a mess.

C   She thought that there was a party at the library, and that no one had invited her.

D   She thought that the library was dangerous.

2. Which event happened LAST in the passage?

A   Nancy makes a list of ways to fix up the library.

B   Nancy's mother helps her plan the cleanup.

C   Nancy's mother thanks her for encouraging everyone to clean up the library.

D   Some of Nancy's friends threw out lots of trash.

3. Read these sentences from the passage.

> Nancy took a long time writing all of her ideas. Her mother came in to check on her.

Which of the following words from these sentences has more than one meaning?

A   took

B   long

C   mother

D   check

4. Explain why Nancy feels proud at the end of the passage. Use details and information from the passage to support your answer.

Now answer numbers 1 through 4. Base your answers on the article "A Change in Plans."

1. Which of these is a theme in this article?

A What is most important in life is having a place to play.

B Building places to play is not very important to adults.

C Parents should always be in charge.

D If people work together, they can solve problems.

2. The section "Parents Propose a Solution" tells about

A the new plan and how it will work.

B the parents and families who will be involved in the new park design.

C Mr. Tang's response to the parents.

D the new basketball courts.

3. The first paragraph tells you

A why it will take a long time to build a new playground.

B why a new playground is needed.

C how to build a new playground.

D how much it will cost to build a new playground.

4. Why can't the construction workers finish the playground quicker?

A They cannot get the materials they need until next summer.

B They have to wait for permits.

C They are busy also working on other projects.

D They will be on vacation.

Write on Demand

PROMPT Do you think the parents thought of a good solution? Why or why not? Use details from the article to support your answer. Write for 8 minutes. Write as much as you can, as well as you can.

The Big Question

How do writers and artists express themselves?

Theme Launcher Video

 LOG ON Find out more about writers and artists at www.macmillanmh.com.

283

How do writers and artists express themselves?

How do you express yourself, or share your thoughts or feelings with others? Some people express themselves through art. In their work you may see if they are worried, excited, or happy. Their work can show the way they see their neighborhood or the world. Some artists sculpt or take photographs.

People also express themselves by writing or telling stories. Writers use their writing in letters, poems, or diaries to express themselves and tell stories.

Research Activities

In this unit you will learn about ways artists and writers express themselves. Research the author of a book you have read or the artist of a piece of art you like. Write about what inspired the artist or author. Write about the time and place in which they lived. Find out as many interesting facts as you can.

Keep Track of Ideas

As you read, keep track of all you are learning about writers and artists and how they express themselves. Use the Study Book to organize and keep track of your ideas. For each week, think about the different ways people express themselves and write them in the correct sections.

FOLDABLES®
Study Organizer

Week 5
Week 4
Week 3
Week 2
Week 1
Unit Theme

Research Toolkit

Conduct Your Unit 3 Research Online with:

Research Roadmap
Follow step-by-step guide to complete your research project.

Online Resources
- Topic Finder and other Research Tools
- Videos and Virtual Fieldtrips
- Photos and Drawings for Presentations
- Related Articles and Web Resources

California Web Site Links

LOG ON Go to **www.macmillanmh.com** for more information.

California People

Kathleen Krull,
Author
Kathleen has loved books since she was a child. She loved them so much she became a writer.

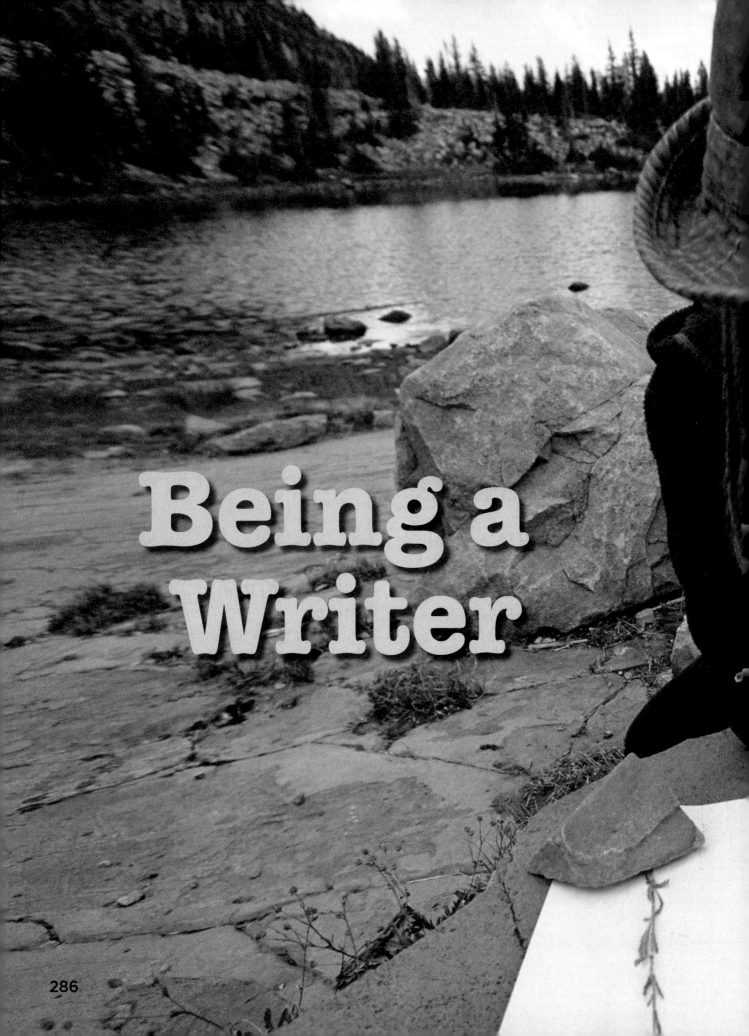

Being a Writer

CA

Talk About It

Why do you think some people like to write? What kinds of things do you like to write about?

LOG ON ▶ Find out more about being a writer at **www.macmillanmh.com**.

Talking to Lulu Delacre, children's author

by Diana Jarvis

Lulu Delacre has written and illustrated many books, including *Golden Tales* and *The Bossy Gallito*. Some of her books have won awards. I wanted to sit and talk with this successful writer.

Q: What were you like at school? Were you **talented**?

A: I was a good student at school. Yes, I was talented. I could see things in a way that I could transfer them onto paper. I loved to draw and create.

Q: Were books always special to you? What is your **single** favorite book?

A: In my house, books had their own special room—my father's study. I loved being in that room. If I have to choose, my favorite book is *Voyage to the Center of the Earth* by Jules Verne.

Q: Writing is difficult. Is there a **proper**, or correct, way to write?

A: I don't believe there's a proper way to write a book. I keep a journal. I draw in it. I also write ideas and things that I find interesting. I reread these journals. At times, a book is born out of these ideas.

Q: Being a writer must be fun. What is the most **excitement** you have ever had as a writer?

A: It was when *The Bossy Gallito* won the Pura Belpré Honor for text and illustration.

Q: What was the first story you sold to a publisher? Tell us about that **acceptance**.

A: Many years ago I created two characters—an elephant named Nathan and his mouse friend named Nicholas Alexander. Out of the sketches I made of these characters, a story was born. Then it was accepted and published.

Q: What is the most **useful** thing kids can do to help their writing?

A: Read, read, read. And keep a journal to write whatever comes into your mind.

Reread for **Comprehension**

Summarize

Author's Purpose An author writes to entertain, inform, or persuade. As you read, stop and summarize what you have read. Then ask yourself, "Why did the author write this information?"

Reread the selection. As you read, look for **clues** to summarize the **author's purpose**. Use the Author's Purpose Chart to help you.

Clues

Author's Purpose

Genre

An **Autobiography** is the story of a person's life written by that person.

✔ **Summarize**

Author's Purpose

As you read, use your Author's Purpose Chart.

Clues

↓

Author's Purpose

Read to Find Out

Why does the author decide to write children's stories?

290

AUTHOR
A TRUE STORY

written and illustrated by
Helen Lester

Award
Winning
Selection

A LONG TIME AGO there lived a three-year-old author. Me. I was the best grocery-list writer in the world and a huge help to my mother. When I wrote a word I knew <u>exactly</u> what it said.

And the fun part was that I could turn each list upside down and the words said the same thing. I think I made hundreds of these **useful** lists for my mother, and she never once said, "No thank you, dear, I have enough."

Then I went to school and learned to make what they called "real letters." My writing was the prettiest in the class, with straight straight lines and round round lines. It was perfect. And it was perfectly backwards.

I didn't just mix up b's and d's. That's easy to do because they look so much alike. My letters started at the right (well, wrong) side of the paper and marched across, pretty as could be—and backwards.

There's a name for somebody with this problem. I was a "mirror writer." My teachers had to hold my work up to a mirror to understand what I had written.

Thanks to a lot of help, I was finally able to write in the **proper** direction. But writing stories was so HARD for me!

Often I couldn't come up with a **single** idea, and my stories got stuck in the middle, and I couldn't think of a title, and I had trouble making the changes my teacher wanted me to make, and I lost my pencils, and I wondered why I was doing this, and I got very very VERY frustrated.

Author's Purpose
Why does the author explain how she used to write as a child?

294

So I spent a lot of time dreaming about what I wanted to be when I grew up. Since no one from the circus came looking for me, I became a teacher. I learned that teachers do not live in schools, eating only crackers and milk and sleeping under their desks.

I also learned that teaching was fun and that children have fantastic imaginations. So my favorite subject to teach was—writing!

One day a friend said, "You should write a children's book."

And I thought, "I spent ten years in second grade, so I know a child from a chicken. Maybe I should."

I went right home and wrote a book. It was the best book I had ever written. Of course, it was the only book I had ever written.

I illustrated it with my nicest drawings and proudly sent it to a publisher. "Lucky people," I thought.

The lucky people sent it back and said, "No thank you." That's called a rejection. I decided I'd never write again.

Until the next day, when I felt better. I wrote a second book and sent it to a different publisher. The second publisher sent the book back. "No thank you." I decided I'd never write again. Until the next day, when I felt better. I wrote another book.

And another.

And another.

And another.

Practice must have helped each story get a little better, for on my seventh try no book came back. Just a "Yes please." That's called an **acceptance**.

I was beside myself with joy and **excitement**. I was the first author I had ever met.

I drew the pictures for my first book. And I did the pictures for this book. But usually I work with an illustrator who has been to art school and who can draw bicycles and refrigerators and pigs. This **talented** person draws what I would if I could.

So here I am. An author! And every time I sit down to write, perfect words line up in perfect order and WHOOP—a perfect book pops out of the computer.

Well, not exactly. Sometimes writing stories is so HARD for me! I can't come up with a single idea, and my stories get stuck in the middle, and I can't think of a title, and I have trouble making the changes my editor wants me to make, and I lose my pencils, and I wonder why I'm doing this, and I get very very VERY frustrated.

But that's sometimes. I love it best when ideas are hatching so fast I can barely write them down. I grab the nearest thing to write on and get so excited I forget what I was doing in the first place. The ideas that come in the middle of the night are hard to read the next day.

Not all of the ideas are useful. I keep a whole box full of fizzled thoughts and half-finished books. I call it my Fizzle Box. Whenever I need an idea, I can go to the box and find wonderful things

—just the name I needed!

—a funny word!

—a wise lesson!

Author's Purpose
Which facts and details on these pages help you figure out the author's purpose?

Usually when I first think a book is finished, it really isn't. I keep going over the story again and again, looking for ways to make it better with little changes here and there. I do this until the book has to be printed. Then it's too late to do anything more!

I used to think that writing had to be done at a special time, while sitting at a desk. But slowly I discovered that I could write <u>any</u>time. And <u>any</u>where. I especially like to write when I'm bored, because then I'm not anymore.

Of course, writing anyTIME anyWHERE sometimes means writing on anyTHING.

Authors are lucky, for they get to meet hundreds of children through letters, school and library visits, and at autographing sessions. I didn't always like autographing books. The first time I autographed, my table was next to the table of a very famous author. I was not a very famous author.

Her line had no end. Mine had no beginning.

I'm glad I didn't join the circus. Even though writing is sometimes hard work, it's what I love to do. I never dreamed I'd become an author. So this is better than a dream come true.

Get Creative
With Helen Lester!

Helen Lester first discovered how much fun writing can be when she was a girl and read her parents' interesting letters. Helen did not think about actually becoming an author until she was a grownup. When she became a mother, Helen read funny books to her children every night. Then she decided to make her own funny books. Helen says that she starts a book whenever a good idea pops into her head. Ideas pop up at really strange times, like when she is at the kitchen sink washing spinach!

Other books by Helen Lester: *Hooway for Wodney Wat* and *Tacky the Penguin*

HELEN LESTER *Illustrated by* LYNN MUNSINGER
HOOWAY FOR WODNEY WAT

TACKY the Penguin
Helen Lester
Illustrated by Lynn Munsinger

LOG ON ▶ Find out more about Helen Lester at **www.macmillanmh.com**.

CA **Author's Purpose**

Helen Lester wrote about her own life. Was her purpose to inform or persuade?

Critical Thinking

Summarize

Use the Author's Purpose Chart to summarize *Author: A True Story.* In your summary, include reasons why the author became a writer.

Clues

↓

Author's Purpose

Think and Compare

1. What clues help you figure out the **author's purpose**? Use story details in your answer. **Summarize: Author's Purpose**

2. Why did the author's friend say that she should write children's books? Use details from the story to support your answer. **Analyze**

3. Can Helen's story help you become a **talented** writer? **Apply**

4. What might have happened if Helen's stories had never been published? Explain. **Synthesize**

5. Read "Talking to Lulu Delacre" on pages 288–289. How would Helen Lester answer these interview questions? In what ways are the two authors' experiences different? **Reading/Writing Across Texts**

Poetry often uses sound words and rhythmic patterns to show strong feelings or describe something.

✔ Literary Elements

Onomatopoeia is a word that sounds like the sound it describes.

Rhythm in a poem is created by a pattern of stressed and unstressed syllables.

LiSTEN

by Bobbi Katz

Libraries have signs like these:

QUIET

DON'T TALK

SILENCE PLEASE

> Read aloud the first four lines and listen for stressed syllables.

By day they're read by me and you.

Mostly we do what the signs tell us to.

Now imagine the library late at night.

The windows are shut and the door's
    locked tight.

But the words in the books are wide awake,

and the noisy words start to itch and ache!

They've been sitting in silence
    on printed pages,

not making a sound for ages and ages.

Suddenly they can't bear the quiet.
They burst out of the books
    in a rackety riot!
splash and splatter –

BANG
BOP
BOOM!

Words bounce and scramble
    through the room.

spitter   sputter

CLANK
CLUNK
CRASH

Clank and *Clunk* are examples of onomatopoeia.

315

buzz **BANG** thunder

splish

splosh

splash

Once words begin to peep and **POP**,
it's clear that they can never stop.
Words that *swizzle*,

snore,

and **SNEEZE**

cannot return to

SILENCE PLEASE

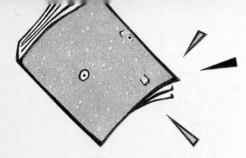

Since noisy words now need new homes,
let them all move into poems!
Poems to sing or read aloud.
Poems that *like* a noisy crowd.

Imagine the library late at night—
     and a riot of words.
Could it happen? It might.

LiSTEN!

ⒸⒶ Critical Thinking

1. Look at the last three words on page 305. Why are they examples of onomatopoeia? **Onomatopoeia**

2. What is the purpose of the signs mentioned in the beginning of the poem? Why is the library noisy? **Analyze**

3. *Author: A True Story* tells about one writer's experiences with words. How might Helen Lester feel about words after reading this poem? **Reading/Writing Across Texts**

LOG ON ▶ Find out more about poetry at **www.macmillanmh.com**.

Reading and Writing Connection

✓ **Capitalization and Punctuation**

Sentences must begin with **capital letters** and have end **punctuation**.

Read the passage below. Notice how author Helen Lester uses complete sentences in her story.

An excerpt from Author, *A True Story*

The author uses complete sentences with the correct capitalization and punctuation so the reader understands her funny story.

So I spent a lot of time dreaming about what I wanted to be when I grew up. Since no one from the circus came looking for me, I became a teacher. I learned that teachers do not live in schools, eating only crackers and milk and sleeping under their desks.

AUTHOR
A TRUE STORY
written and illustrated by
Helen Lester

Read and Find

Read Jazmin's writing below. What does she do to help you read her sentences easily? Use the tips below to help you.

A Giant Meal
by Jazmin M.

Mmmmm! The smell of turkey wafted into my room where I was playing. My stomach growled just as mom called us to dinner. Spread out in front of us was the most food I had ever seen. Plate upon plate of mashed potatoes, stuffing, cranberry sauce, and more made my mouth water.

Read about a special family meal.

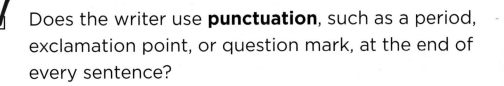

Writer's Checklist

✓ Does the writer put a **capital letter** at the beginning of every sentence?

✓ Does the writer use **punctuation**, such as a period, exclamation point, or question mark, at the end of every sentence?

☑ Are you able to easily understand where Jazmin's sentences start and stop?

WRITING LETTERS

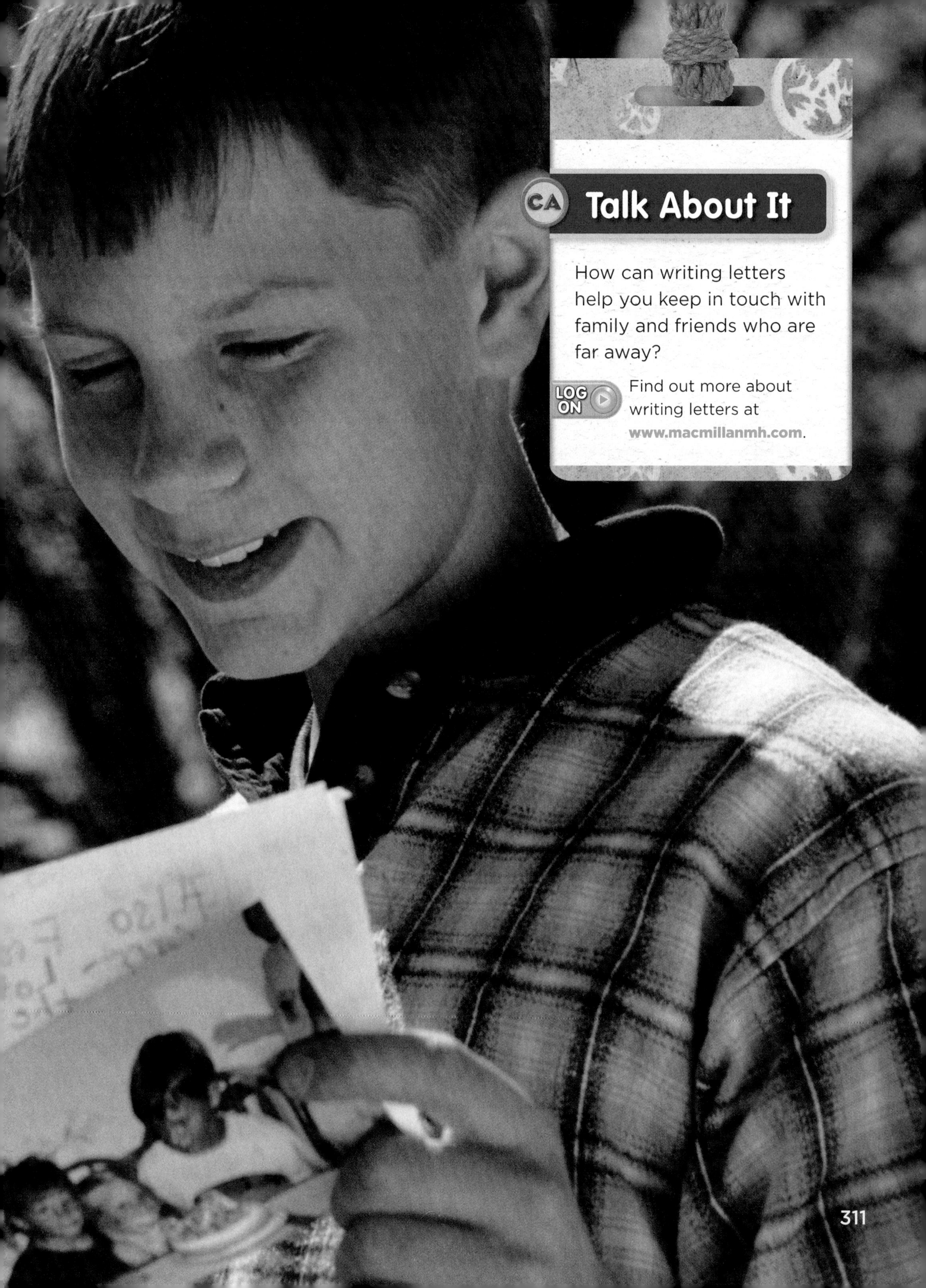

Talk About It

How can writing letters help you keep in touch with family and friends who are far away?

LOG ON Find out more about writing letters at **www.macmillanmh.com**.

Mail for Matty

by Susan Tanner

Nana has been visiting for two weeks, but now it's time for her to go home. I wish she could stay.

At the Airport

"Why so sad, Matty? I'm going home, not to the moon!" joked Nana.

"Miami's so far away, it might as well be the moon," I answered. I tightened my hold on Nana's plane ticket until it began to **crackle**.

Nana laughed. "Oh, it's not that far! You'll see me soon," she said. "I promise."

Just then a voice on the loudspeaker **announced** that Nana's flight was boarding.

"Time to go," said Nana. "When I get home, I'll send you a surprise. Watch for it!" She hugged us good-bye. We waited until her plane **soared** up high into the dark but **starry** sky. I wondered what my surprise was.

312

Waiting for the Surprise

When I got home, I kept checking the door and looking out the window for my surprise. Then Dad called, "Hey, Matty, come over here!"

Dad was at the computer. Matty **noticed** a picture of an envelope on the screen. I had e-mail! The title of the e-mail said "Surprise!" It read:

Dear Matty,

Uncle Pete set up my new computer while I was gone. Now we can send e-mails every day. Can you see the photograph I sent? It's a picture of me. I told you you'd see me soon! Write back.

Hugs and kisses,

Nana

Nana did surprise me! I'm so excited that I can talk to her every day.

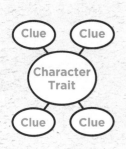

Surprise!

To: matty@example.com
Cc:
Subject: Surprise!

Dear Matty,
Uncle Pete set up my new computer while I was gone. Now we can send e-mails every day. Can you see the photograph I sent? It's a picture of me. I told you you'd see me soon! Write back.
Hugs and kisses,
Nana

Reread for **Comprehension**

Analyze Story Structure

Character, Setting, Plot Characters, setting, and plot make up a story's structure. The main character is the person who the story is mostly about. An author uses character actions and **character traits**, or personality, to develop a story's plot.

Reread the selection and write **clues** about Matty's character on your Character Web. Think about Matty's actions and thoughts after Nana leaves.

Clue   Clue

Character
Trait

Clue   Clue

Genre

Realistic Fiction is an invented story that could have happened in real life.

Analyze Story Structure

Character, Setting, Plot
As you read, use your Character Web.

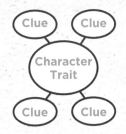

Read to Find Out

How does Juno communicate with his grandmother?

Dear Juno

by Soyung Pak
illustrated by
Susan Kathleen Hartung

Award Winning Author and Illlustrator

Juno watched as the red and white blinking lights **soared** across the night sky like shooting stars, and waited as they disappeared into faraway places. Juno wondered where they came from. He wondered where they were going. And he wondered if any of the planes came from a little town near Seoul where his grandmother lived, and where she ate persimmons every evening before bed.

Juno looked at the letter that came that day. It was long and white and smudged. He saw the red and blue marks on the edges and knew the letter came from far away. His name and address were neatly printed on the front, so he knew the letter was for him. But best of all, the special stamp on the corner told Juno that the letter was from his grandmother.

> **Character**
> What do Juno's thoughts and actions tell you about him?

Through the window Juno could see his parents. He saw bubbles growing in the sink. He saw dirty dishes waiting to be washed. He knew he would have to wait for the cleaning to be done before his parents could read the letter to him.

"Maybe I can read the inside, too," Juno said to his dog, Sam. Sam wagged his tail. Very carefully, Juno opened the envelope. Inside, he found a letter folded into a neat, small square.

He unfolded it. Tucked inside were a picture and a dried flower.

Juno looked at the letters and words he couldn't understand. He pulled out the photograph. It was a picture of his grandmother holding a cat. He pulled out the red and yellow flower. It felt light and gentle like a dried leaf. Juno smiled. "C'mon, Sam," Juno said. "Let's find Mom and Dad."

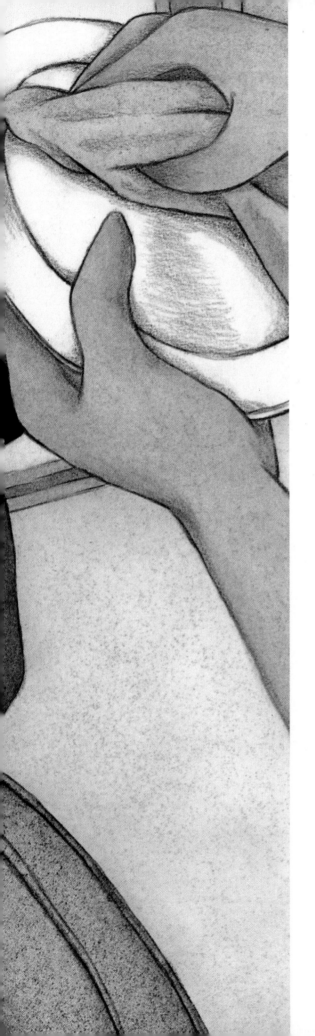

"Grandma has a new cat," Juno said as he handed the letter to his mother. "And she's growing red and yellow flowers in her garden."

"How do you know she has a new cat?" Juno's father asked.

"She wouldn't send me a picture of a strange cat," said Juno.

"I guess not," said Juno's father.

"How do you know the flower is from her garden?" asked Juno's mother.

"She wouldn't send me a flower from someone else's garden," Juno answered.

"No, she wouldn't," said Juno's mother.

Then Juno's mother read him the letter.

Character
What clues tell you that Juno is smart?

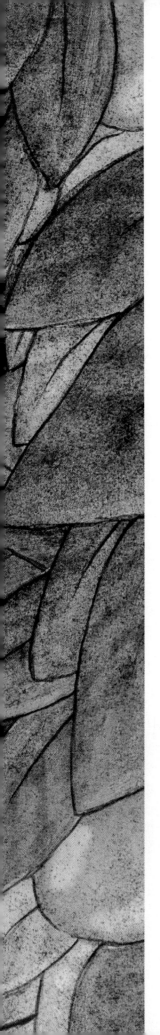

Dear Juno,

How are you? I have a new cat to keep me company. I named him Juno after you. He can't help me weed, but the rabbits no longer come to eat my flowers.

Grandma

"Just like you read it yourself," Juno's father said.

"I did read it," Juno said.

"Yes, you did," said his mother.

At school, Juno showed his class his grandmother's picture and dried flower. His teacher even pinned the letter to the board. All day long, Juno kept peeking at the flower from his grandmother's garden. He didn't have a garden that grew flowers, but he had a swinging tree.

Juno looked at the letter pinned to the board. Did his grandmother like getting letters, too? Yes, Juno thought. She likes getting letters just like I do. So Juno decided to write one.

After school, Juno ran to his backyard. He picked a leaf from the swinging tree— the biggest leaf he could find.

Juno found his mother, who was sitting at her desk. He showed her the leaf. "I'm going to write a letter," he told her.

"I'm sure it will be a very nice letter," she answered, and gave him a big yellow envelope.

"Yes it will," Juno said, and then he began to draw.

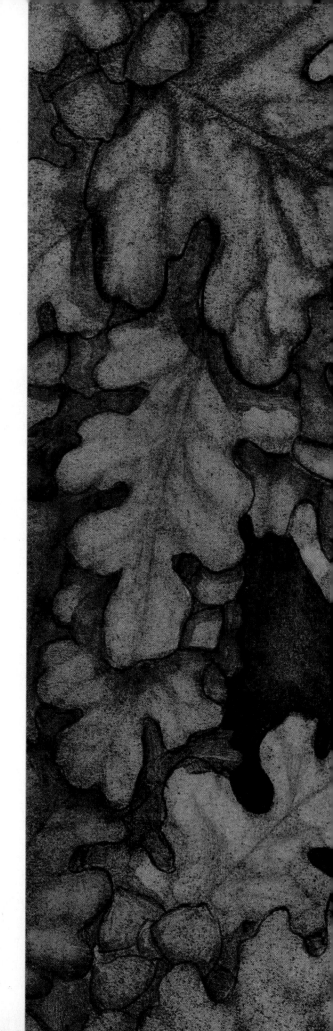

First, he drew a picture of his mom and dad standing outside the house. Second, he drew a picture of Sam playing underneath his big swinging tree. Then very carefully, Juno drew a picture of himself standing under an airplane in a **starry**, nighttime sky. After he was finished, he placed everything in the envelope.

"Here's my letter," Juno **announced** proudly. "You can read it if you want."

Juno's father looked in the envelope.

He pulled out the leaf. "Only a big swinging tree could grow a leaf this big," he said.

Juno's mother pulled out one of the drawings. "What a fine picture," she said. "It takes a good artist to say so much with a drawing."

Juno's father patted Juno on the head. "It's just like a real letter," he said.

"It is a real letter," Juno said.

"It certainly is," said his mother. Then they mailed the envelope and waited.

One day a big envelope came. It was from Juno's grandmother. This time, Juno didn't wait at all. He opened the envelope right away.

Inside, Juno found a box of colored pencils. He knew she wanted another letter.

Next, he pulled out a picture of his grandmother.
He **noticed** she was sitting with a cat and two kittens.
He thought for a moment and laughed. Now his
grandmother would have to find a new name for her
cat—in Korea, Juno was a boy's name, not a girl's.

Then he pulled out a small toy plane.

Juno smiled. His grandmother was coming to visit.

"Maybe she'll bring her cat when she comes to visit," Juno said to Sam as he climbed into bed. "Maybe you two will be friends."

Soon Juno was fast asleep. And when he dreamed that night, he dreamed about a faraway place, a village just outside Seoul, where his grandmother, whose gray hair sat on top of her head like a powdered doughnut, was sipping her morning tea.

The cool air feels crisp against her cheek. Crisp enough to **crackle**, he dreams, like the golden leaves which cover the persimmon garden.

Letters to
Soyung and Susan

Author

Soyung Pak was born in South Korea, but she does not remember very much about it. She moved to the United States when she was just two years old. Like Juno,

Soyung had a grandmother who lived in South Korea. Soyung remembers playing in her American backyard. It was a lot like Juno's yard, with a nice, big tree.

Other books by Soyung Pak: *A Place to Grow* and *Sumi's First Day of School Ever*

Illustrator

Susan Kathleen Hartung says she's been drawing ever since she could hold a crayon. Unlike Juno, who used paper, Susan would draw on any surface she could find. Susan's parents were not too happy about that. But when they saw how much she loved to draw, they encouraged her to study art.

LOG ON ▶ Find out more about Soyung Pak and Susan Kathleen Hartung at **www.macmillanmh.com**.

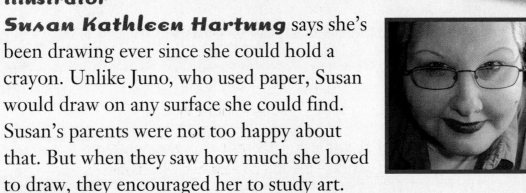

CA Author's Purpose

What clues can you use to figure out Soyung Pak's purpose for writing *Dear Juno*? Did the author want to entertain or inform?

Critical Thinking

Summarize

Use your Character Web to help you summarize *Dear Juno*. Describe the characters of Juno and his grandmother based on things they did in the story.

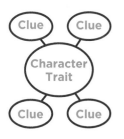

Think and Compare

1. How do the **characters** Juno and his grandmother feel about each other? How does this affect the **plot**? Use details from the story in your answer. **Analyze Story Structure: Character, Setting, Plot**

2. Juno wanted to read his grandmother's letters. How does he figure out what is written in her letters? Use story details and examples in your answer. **Evaluate**

3. If you **announced** to your friends that you were moving away, what objects would you want them to send you? How would this help you to keep in touch? **Apply**

4. What are some problems that can happen when relatives live far from each other? Explain your answer. **Analyze**

5. Read "Mail for Matty" on pages 312–313. How are Matty and Juno alike? How are they both surprised at the end of each story? Use details from both selections in your answer. **Reading/Writing Across Texts**

Genre

Nonfiction gives information about real people, places, or things.

Text Feature

A Time Line shows the time order in which events happened.

Content Vocabulary

technology	improved
communicate	images

How We Keep in Touch

by Eric Michaels

When your great-grandparents were young, the world was very different. People did not have the kind of **technology** that we have today to **communicate** with each other. Things such as cell phones and computers were not yet invented. It took longer for people to get news to each other.

Today's technology makes it easier and faster to stay close to people.

How Communicating Has Changed

Reading a Time Line

Read the time line from left to right. Use the dates to find out when events took place.

1800　　　　**1850**

1843–1844

First telegraph line built

1843

First fax machine

1860–1861

Mail delivered by Pony Express

Back Then

Long ago, people wrote letters to stay in touch. From 1860–1861, some letters were carried by the Pony Express. Only the fastest horseback riders were hired to carry letters and packages across the country. Then trains began to carry the mail from city to city. By the early 1900s, airplanes were a faster way to carry mail across the country and around the world.

Sometimes a message had to reach someone almost immediately. Telegraphs were machines that could send signals in a special code over an electric line.

1900   **1950**   **2000**

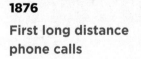

1876

First long distance phone calls

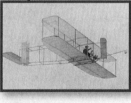

1911

First airmail flight in the U.S.

1973

First cell phone call

1975–1977

First personal computers

1990s

First personal computers link to the Internet

Here and Now

As times changed, the tools we use to communicate have **improved**. New inventions have made it easy to contact friends and family within seconds!

Telephones came into use in the late 1800s. They were very different from the phones you use now. Early phones did not have dials. Many people shared phone lines with others. The shared lines were called party lines.

Modern phones can do so many things. Wireless phones can be carried with us wherever we travel. Some phones let you play games, get text messages, and even take pictures! These **images** can be sent to other wireless phones.

The fax machine was patented in 1843, but it came into regular use in the 1930s. A fax machine sends images on paper as electric signals. Then another machine receives the signals and prints them. Many offices and homes have fax machines.

Computers have made some of the biggest changes in communication. The Internet sends e-mail messages around the world in seconds! Some families have their own Web sites. They can post pictures and family news so everyone can be kept up to date.

Although new technology helps us stay in touch with each other, many people still enjoy sending and getting letters. With so many ways to communicate, it's easy to find your favorite way to keep in touch.

 Critical Thinking

1. Look at the time line on pages 340–341. Which inventions became popular between the years 1950 and 2000? **Reading a Time Line**

2. Why do you think so many people now use computers to stay in touch with one another? **Analyze**

3. Think about this article and *Dear Juno*. In what other ways could Juno and his grandmother have communicated with each other? **Reading/Writing Across Texts**

 History/Social Science Activity

Do research and create a time line with important dates to show how the telephone has changed from the 1800s to the present day.

 Find out more about communication at **www.macmillanmh.com**.

Writing

CA

✓ Capitalization and Punctuation

Using correct capitalization and punctuation helps the reader read your writing easily with the right expression.

Read the passage below. Notice how author Soyung Pak uses complete sentences in her story.

An excerpt from
Dear Juno

The author uses capital letters and end punctuation to help us read her sentences easily. The capital letter shows us where a new thought starts and the end punctuation shows us where it ends.

Juno looked at the letter that came that day. It was long and white and smudged. He saw the red and blue marks on the edges and knew the letter came from far away. His name and address were neatly printed on the front, so he knew the letter was for him. But best of all, the special stamp on the corner told Juno that the letter was from his grandmother.

Dear Juno
by Soyung Pak
Illustrated by
Susan Kathleen Hartung

Read and Find

Read Tarik's writing below. What did he do to help you read his sentences easily? Use the tips below to help you.

The Fort

by Tarik L.

Kenny and I built a fort in my backyard yesterday. We worked together to stack cardboard boxes higher than our heads! Kenny lifted them on top of each other, while I taped the boxes together.

Read about how I helped build a fort.

Writer's Checklist

✔ Does the writer put a **capital letter** at the beginning of every sentence?

✔ Does the writer use **punctuation**, such as a period, exclamation point, or question mark, at the end of every sentence?

☑ Are you able to easily understand where Tarik's sentences start and stop?

What are some different types of tools that people use to communicate with each other?

 Find out more about communication at www.macmillanmh.com.

Let's
COMMUNICATE

High-Tech Bullies

Twelve-year-old Mariah Lopez had a problem. First, girls in school started a mean rumor about her. Then, Mariah started to get text messages with disturbing content. Finally, she got threatening calls from numbers she didn't know. Mariah needed help.

Today's bullies have gone high tech in **record** numbers. They threaten others through e-mail or instant messages. They post hurtful words on Web sites. They use cell phones to send nasty texts.

E-bullies are on the rise. One third of kids surveyed in a recent study said they had been cyberbullied. Experts **estimate** that girls are twice as likely as boys to be victims of cyberbullies.

To help solve the problem, many states are working on laws to ban cyberbullying. They want schools to punish students who do it. Mariah's school district added cyberbullying to its anti-bullying rules.

After Mariah got her parents and principal involved, the cyberbullies were caught and they apologized.

Polls estimate that more than 13 million kids have been cyberbullied.

C U L8R, Bullies

Follow these tips to help you stay safe from cyberbullies.

• Don't give out personal information on the Internet.

• Watch what you write and record on video. Make sure you don't say things that are hurtful to others.

• Block unwanted messages or phone numbers.

• Do not reply to any messages or IMs that make you uncomfortable.

• Keep a record. Print any harmful material you receive.

• If cyberbullying continues, let an adult know.

Top Things Kids do on the Internet

Here's a look at what kids ages 12 to 17 **focus** their attention on when they're online.

Activity	Percentage of kids online
Send or read e-mail	89%
Play games	81%
Get news or information	76%
Send or receive instant messages	75%
Buy things, such as books, music, or clothing	43%
Send or receive text messages with a cell phone	38%

Source: Pew Internet Project

 LOG ON Find out more about online safety at **www.macmillanmh.com**.

Messaging Mania

Do you know what these mean?

"Wass^?"   "N2M, U?"
"JC."   "G2G. BFN."

If you figured it out, you probably use instant messaging, or IM. It lets people "talk" to each other in real time. Instant messages are typed very fast. Users usually don't slow down to capitalize or spell out words. As a result, users keep inventing shorter versions of words and IM slang.

Kids are logging on and sounding off. Will it change friendships and the English language?

hey, mike!

hey julia! wass^???

nm, u???

n2m either jc, doin homework BLAH...brb

ShoppingDiva01

sup jake?

hey nm jc u???

jc...can't wait til Saturday

y?

goin to c Crazy Cats play

HiTeckerrr

Crazy Cats?!! No way —they r totally my fave right now!

i have xtra tix...

Srsly???!!! Oooooo, wld b GR8!!!

well let me no asap, julia on 2, an i know she likes 'em

askin now. Brb.

MrPopular5000

CAN YOU BELIEVE JEN DIDNT INVITE ME TO HER PARTY?!

she only invited 3 ppl ...her mom wouldnt let ne1 else come.

but i invited her 2 ALL my parties! so bummed! y wuznt I invited?!!

maybe u should ask jen

y should i??? if she doesnt want me at her party, im not speaking 2 her!!!!

GoodGirl109

Shhh don't tell her I'm here.

Jen

SupaStar2003

Keyboard Nation

The Internet is a quick and easy way to exchange up-to-the-minute gossip with others. Studies **estimate** that most IM sessions last more than half an hour. Many kids say they IM friends every day.

Wrong Message?

Instant messaging seems to be a great tool for communication, but it can cause problems. For example, sometimes kids include negative feelings in their messages and they end up hurting someone, or even losing a friend. "I can express my emotions more easily without having the guilt of saying it face-to-face," says Oliver Davies, of Palo Alto, California.

Also, unlike people in face-to-face conversations, most IMers can't interpret facial expressions. This makes communication between people confusing, and sometimes difficult. When a sender does not think about how the receiver might react to written words, useful communication can break down.

To avoid these problems, kids should remember to only write things on IM that they would feel comfortable saying in person. Also, kids should think about how their readers might react to their words.

351

It's About Time

There are other reasons why cyber conversations aren't always good for kids. Many parents and teachers are not happy with their kids' IM habits. Spending too much time on the computer can lead to too little time exercising, playing outdoors, or studying. Julia Long of Washington, says that it's hard for her son to **focus** on homework when he's waiting for an IM. Kids' safety is another concern.

The solution to all these problems for many parents is to keep an eye on IMing. Parents may cut down their kids' time online. They may put the computer in a common area of the house. This way they can pay more attention to the content of the online talk.

IM Not So Bad

Researchers who study the Internet say IMs are okay for kids. The researchers note that new technology often makes adults nervous. In the past, adults complained about the effects of television and video games on kids. Now they say the same thing about the Internet.

Most teachers get upset when IM slang and emoticons (made with punctuation marks) show up in kids' writing. The habit of writing in IM language often makes its way into essays and other places where more formal language should be used.

Get the Message!

Here are some common IM abbreviations.

bfn	bye for now
brb	be right back
g2g	got to go
jc	just chillin'
l8r	later
lol	laugh out loud
nm	not much
oic	oh, I see
rly	really
sry	sorry
sup; wass^	what's up?
ur	your or you're

Some adults fear that kids won't learn correct English because of IM. But Naomi Baron, a professor at American University in Washington, D.C., disagrees. She says that won't happen if teachers get kids to understand the difference between proper English and spoken English.

In fact, IMing might make kids better students. Typing a computer note to friends improves writing skills. It also helps kids learn to type. They may get fast enough to break a speed-typing **record**!

"Language has always changed, and it always will," Naomi Baron told TFK. "It must change as the things we do and the things we encounter change."

What a relief! G2G. L8R.

CA Critical Thinking

1. What is one **problem** that some teachers fear users of IM will have? What is the **solution**?

2. What are some benefits of using Instant Messaging?

3. Do you think Instant Messaging is the best way for friends to communicate? Explain your answer.

4. What is one thing about Instant Messaging that both "High-Tech Bullies" and "Messaging Mania" say you should avoid?

Steven Mintz, 13, likes IMing friends. "I can talk to more people at once," he notes. Chatting online is also a good way to keep up with friends who live far away. Kids don't have to worry about running up the phone bill."

Gabbi Lewin, 12, of Dallas, Texas, says that she's on instant messenger almost every day. She adds that without it "there would be no way to communicate. Our parents are on the phone all the time."

WRITE ON!

Think and Search

The answer is in more than one place. Keep reading to find the answer.

Computers make it easy for kids to write.

Nowadays you don't need to be a famous author for people to read your stories. All it takes is a click of the mouse.

More and more kids are writing for the Internet. Many schools have online literary magazines or writing projects to encourage its students' online publishing practices. Outside school, kids write blogs. A blog is a Web log, or online diary. Writing and publishing stories online gives kids another way to express themselves.

The Internet makes it easy for people to read stories. Sometimes people can review other people's online stories. A good review makes many kids want to practice their writing.

Fictional stories are gaining popularity with young writers. Many kids make themselves the hero of a story. Other writers create fantasy stories about famous people, real or fictional. These types of stories are called fan fiction. Some writing Web sites have only fan fiction.

Xing Li, a computer programmer from Los Angeles, started a fan fiction Web site for young writers. "I know how hard these writers work, and I respect it," Li says. He wants beginning writers to find an audience and perfect their words.

Go on ▶

Directions: Now answer Numbers 1–5. Base your answers on the article "Write On!"

1. **What kind of writing do kids do for the Internet?**

    A   only nonfiction such as blogs

    B   only fictional stories such as fan fiction

    C   fiction, blogs, and story reviews

    D   reviews and online diaries but no fiction

2. **When kids write stories for the Internet, they**

    A   get to put their thoughts and ideas into words.

    B   earn money by selling their stories online.

    C   get the chance to know many famous authors.

    D   learn how to set up fan fiction Web sites.

Tip

Look for information in more than one place.

3. **An example of fan fiction is**

    A   a poem about your family.

    B   a real story about a famous person.

    C   a fantasy story about a cartoon character.

    D   a biography of a famous person.

4. **How are blogs and fan fiction alike? How are they different?**

5. **How have computers and the Internet changed the way many people write and publish stories? Use details from the article to support your answer.**

✎ Write on Demand

CA Most people have something that is important to them.

Think about a thing that is important to you.

Write a letter <u>to a friend</u> to explain why it is important.

Letters should include a date, proper salutation, body, closing, and signature.

A letter may be personal or formal. Clue words, such as <u>to a friend</u>, help you figure out your audience.

Below, see how one student begins a response to the prompt above.

The writer tells his friend why the glove is important.

May 20

Dear José:
    My favorite thing is a baseball glove. It is very old. Parts of it are worn out, but it is still important to me. My dad gave it to me last summer. He used the glove when he was in third grade. My glove is more than 20 years old!
    Someday I will let you use my special glove, too!
    Your friend,
    Marcos

Writing Prompt

Respond in writing to the prompt below. Write for

8 minutes. Write as much as you can, as well as you can.

Review the hints below before and after you write.

CA Most people have friends who are special to them.

Think about a friend you have and what interesting

information you could share.

Now write a letter to explain this interesting information.

Writing Hints for Prompts

- ☑ Read the prompt carefully.
- ☑ Plan your writing by organizing your ideas.
- ☑ Support your ideas by telling more about each event or reason.
- ☑ Use complete sentences and proper letter format.
- ☑ Choose words that help others understand what you mean.
- ☑ Review and edit your writing for correct capitalization and punctuation.

Being an Artist

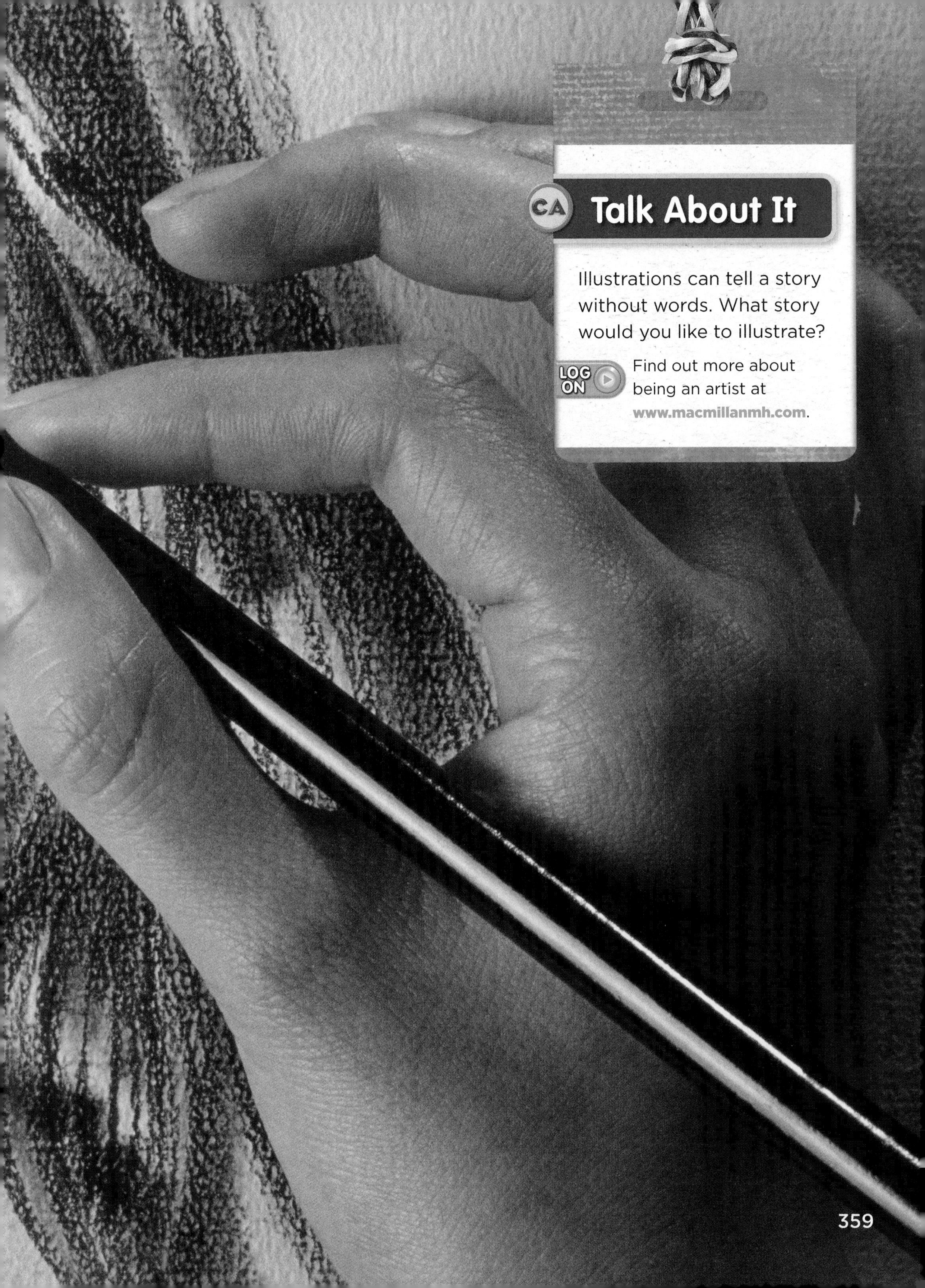

Talk About It

Illustrations can tell a story without words. What story would you like to illustrate?

LOG ON Find out more about being an artist at **www.macmillanmh.com**.

Vocabulary

instance   textures

illustrate   sketches

style   suggestions

Context Clues

Sentence Clues are words or phrases in surrounding sentences that help you figure out the meaning of an unfamiliar word.

What sentence clues help you figure out the meaning of *sketches*?

Cave painting found in Lascaux, France

DRAW!

by Jesse Howes

Artists draw on different types of materials. For **instance**, artists have used walls, paper, and computers.

CAVE DRAWINGS

The first paintings of horses and other animals were found on cave walls. Scientists think they were made 30,000 years ago.

Why did people **illustrate** cave walls? Before there was paper, artists used what they had—rock!

DRAWING ON PAPER

Paper was invented about 2,000 years ago. Depending on what it's made of, paper can have a unique **style**, with different colors and **textures**. It can be plain white or a pattern of different colors, and smooth or bumpy. Plus, it's easier to carry than cave walls!

ANIMATION

About 100 years ago, artists used flipbooks to make moving pictures. Flipbooks are collections of **sketches** placed one on top of the other. Each sketch is a bit different. When the pages are flipped, the drawings seem to move. Next, a camera was used to take pictures of the drawings to make a film.

Today, some artists use computers to draw. They can even draw special effects for video games. Illustration has come a long way in 30,000 years!

TRY IT YOURSELF

Do you need **suggestions** for what to do in your free time? Make a flipbook. Then flip the pages quickly so you can watch it like a movie.

Reread for **Comprehension**

Analyze Text Structure

Sequence Some articles are organized in time order. One way to analyze a text's structure is to look for a **sequence** of events. The signal words *first, next, then, after, finally, later, today,* and *at the same time* tell you the order in which **events** take place. Reread the selection. Use your Sequence Chart to find the sequence of events.

Event

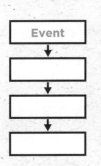

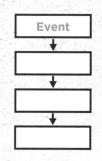

Comprehension

Genre

Narrative Nonfiction is a story about actual events, living things, or people.

Analyze Text Structure

Sequence

As you read, use your Sequence Chart.

```
┌──────────────┐
│    Event     │
└──────┬───────┘
       ↓
┌──────────────┐
│              │
└──────┬───────┘
       ↓
┌──────────────┐
│              │
└──────┬───────┘
       ↓
┌──────────────┐
│              │
└──────────────┘
```

Read to Find Out

How do illustrators decide what art to create for a book?

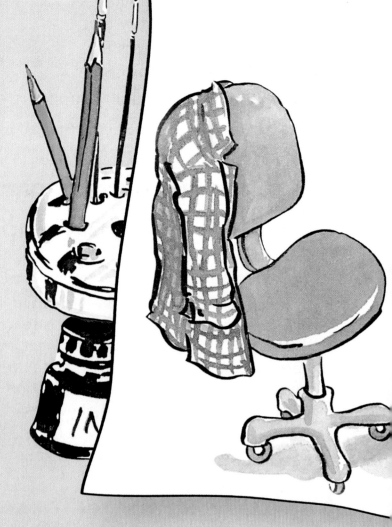

What Do Illustrators Do?

written and illustrated by

EILEEN CHRISTELOW

Award Winning Author and Illustrator

What do illustrators do? They tell stories with pictures.

This picture shows where two illustrators live and work.

Suppose those two illustrators each decided to **illustrate** *Jack and the Beanstalk*. Would they tell the story the same way? Would they draw the same kind of pictures?

I'm going to retell and illustrate JACK AND THE BEANSTALK. Go lie down, Scooter! I'll take you for a walk later.

I've been asked to illustrate JACK AND THE BEANSTALK. Go away, Leonard!

First, illustrators decide which scenes in the story they want to illustrate …

A plan shows which pictures go on which pages.

After illustrators make a plan for their book, they need to make a dummy. (A dummy is a model of the book.) First they decide what shape and size the book will be.

Then they make **sketches** of the pictures that will go on each page of the dummy.

The first sketches are often rough scribbles on tracing paper.

Sequence
What do illustrators do first?
What do they do next?

As they are sketching, illustrators need to decide how things will look: the characters, their clothes, the setting.

Illustrators can use their imaginations or they may have to do some research.

Some illustrators are also authors. They can change their story as they work on the sketches.

Each illustration has a different problem. For **instance**: From what point of view do you draw the magic bean being planted?

Should I draw this picture from a bird's-eye view? Close up? Far away? A mouse's-eye view?

The close up, bird's-eye view shows the bean best.

The mouse can't see the bean at all.

How do you draw a beanstalk so it
looks like it's growing?

There is usually more than one way to solve the same problem.

Here is another problem: How do
you make a beanstalk look really TALL?

If the giant doesn't look BIG enough or SCARY enough, the illustrator will draw that picture again.

How would it feel to run across a table right under the nose of a sleeping GIANT?

Illustrators need to draw how their characters feel. (Sometimes they make faces in a mirror to see how an expression would look.)

Sometimes illustrators need
someone else to model for them.

Each illustrator has a different **style** of drawing, just as every person has a different style of handwriting.

We're trying a new style.

The giant . . . Big BOB

Jack . . . Jack Trumper

Jack's mom . . . Ethel Trumper

Jacqueline . . . Jacqueline

Different styles for drawing Jack and Jacqueline

When illustrators have finished their dummies, they show them to the editor and the designer at the publishing company.

The editor decides whether the pictures tell the story.

I love your illustrations! But Jack looks too old at the end of the book. And on page 21 the giant doesn't look mean enough.

Okay, those things should be easy to fix.

If she loves his book, why *does* she want him to change it?

She's just suggesting ways to make it better!

The designer makes **suggestions** about the design of the book.

She chooses the typeface for the words and the cover.

Sequence
What happens after the dummy is finished?

377

Illustrators need to decide how they want to do the finished illustrations.

They can draw different kinds of lines and **textures** with different kinds of tools.

I'm trying different kinds of lines . . . pencil, pen, brush.

pencil

brush

pen with flexible point

felt tip pen

They can color their illustrations with paint, pastels, pencils, or crayons …

They can do an illustration without any black line at all!

I'm experimenting. I've tried watercolors, watercolor crayons, and colored pencils.

watercolors

watercolor crayons

colored pencils

Illustrators need to choose the paper they want to use for their finished illustrations.

Some papers are good for watercolor, others for pastel, others for pencil ... Some are smooth. Some are textured.

Sometimes illustrators throw away their pictures and start again.

Sometimes they change the colors.

Or they may change the composition.

It can take months to finish all the illustrations for a picture book.

Before they are sent to the publisher, they need to be checked to make sure nothing is left out.

Illustrators often do the cover of the book last. The cover tells a lot about a story: What is it about? Does it look interesting?

The cover is a clue to how the illustrator will tell the story.

Would these covers make you want to read the books?

What Does Eileen Christelow Do?

Eileen Christelow had a very strange dream when she was just three years old. She dreamed she could read! In first grade, she really did learn to read. From then on, Eileen's nose was almost always in a book.

As Eileen grew up, she discovered art and photography. She liked to look at children's books and thought about writing and illustrating her own. After a lot of hard work, Eileen's first book was published. Eileen gets her story ideas from newspapers, the radio, and even conversations.

Other books by Eileen Christelow: *Five Little Monkeys Jumping on the Bed* and *What Do Authors Do?*

 LOG ON ▶ Find out more about Eileen Christelow at **www.macmillanmh.com**.

CA Author's Purpose

Did Eileen Christelow write to entertain or inform readers? What clues help you to figure out why she wrote *What Do Illustrators Do?*

 Critical Thinking

Summarize

Use your Sequence Chart to help you summarize *What Do Illustrators Do?* Tell how to illustrate a book by telling the steps in time order.

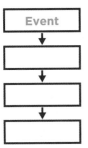

Event
↓
↓
↓

Think and Compare

1. What is the **sequence** of events that happens before an illustrator makes dummy **sketches**? Use details from the story in your answer. **Analyze Text Structure: Sequence**

2. Reread page 367 of *What Do Illustrators Do?* How is an author/illustrator's job different from an illustrator's job? How are they alike? Use story details in your answer. **Analyze**

3. Which illustrator's book would you enjoy more: the traditional story of Jack and the Beanstalk or the story with Jacqueline? Give reasons for your answer. **Evaluate**

4. What traits does a person need in order to become an illustrator? **Apply**

5. Read "Draw!" on pages 360–361. How is it similar to *What Do Illustrators Do?* How are the two stories different? Use details from both selections in your answer. **Reading/Writing Across Texts**

What Does Eileen Do?

She Illustrates!

Jobs in Animation

by Lisa Soo

Animators are artists. Their drawings seem to come to life because the characters move in their animation. Once upon a time, animators worked only on movies. They drew pictures on cards that were flipped in front of the camera to make the characters move. Then computers came along. This new **technology** helps animators draw, color, and move their creations better than ever before!

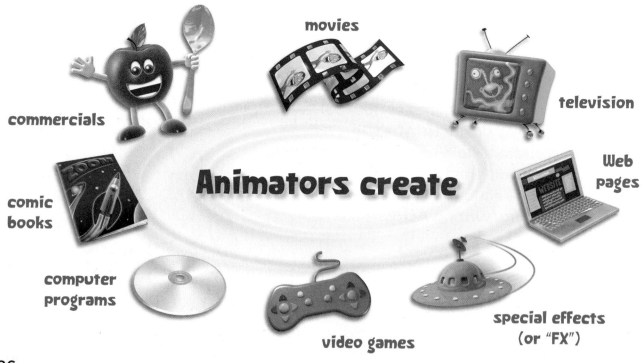

commercials

movies

television

comic books

Animators create

Web pages

computer programs

video games

special effects (or "FX")

Today some animators still draw by hand. It takes thousands of drawings to make an animated film this way. There's a lot more to animating than just drawing. It takes a whole team to get the job done. There are people who write the story and people who draw. Others fill in color or add sound.

Reading an Interview

An interview is a written record of a conversation. Speaker tags show who is talking.

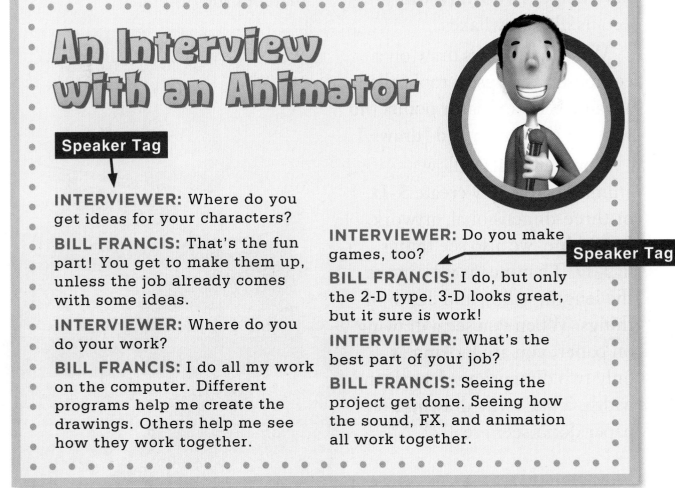

An Interview with an Animator

Speaker Tag

INTERVIEWER: Where do you get ideas for your characters?

BILL FRANCIS: That's the fun part! You get to make them up, unless the job already comes with some ideas.

INTERVIEWER: Where do you do your work?

BILL FRANCIS: I do all my work on the computer. Different programs help me create the drawings. Others help me see how they work together.

INTERVIEWER: Do you make games, too?

Speaker Tag

BILL FRANCIS: I do, but only the 2-D type. 3-D looks great, but it sure is work!

INTERVIEWER: What's the best part of your job?

BILL FRANCIS: Seeing the project get done. Seeing how the sound, FX, and animation all work together.

Telling the Story

It all starts with a story. A director usually comes up with an idea. Then a writer writes a **script**. This tells how the characters, settings, and events take shape. Next comes the **storyboard**. An artist draws the story and puts the pictures up on large boards. Then the writer puts the words with the pictures.

Drawing and Coloring

Animators draw the characters. They also draw any important moving objects. Some animators have helpers who draw tiny details like snowflakes.

When animators draw on a computer, they use a tool called a wand. The animator points the wand at the screen and "draws."

Computers also allow animators to easily create **3-D**, or three-dimensional, artwork. In real life, we also see things in 3-D. That means we can see the length, width, and depth of things. When you see a drawing on paper, you are looking at only two dimensions: length and width. That's why drawings on paper don't seem real!

The 3 Dimensions

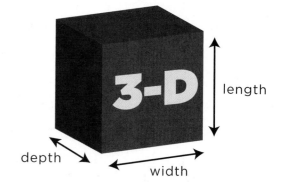

length

depth

width

Background Artists

Some artists draw only the story's setting, or background art. Others work only on the colors. They review the colors animators have used, and they make sure the same shades of colors are used so each picture matches the others.

Finishing the Job

The sound team hires actors to be the voices for the characters. The actors read from the scripts. Their voices are recorded and replayed to match the animated pictures. Other members of the sound team add sound effects, such as ringing bells and music.

The drawings, color, story, voices, and music come together in the end to make an animated film. Whether it's a half-hour cartoon or a feature-length movie, you can be sure that a lot of people worked hard to get it to your screen.

 Critical Thinking

1. Reread the interview on page 387. Name three things you learned about Bill Francis's job. **Reading an Interview**

2. Based on what you read, would you like to be an animator? Why or why not? **Evaluate**

3. Think about *What Do Illustrators Do?* and this article. How are the jobs of illustrator and animator alike? How are they different? **Reading/Writing Across Texts**

 History/Social Science Activity

Think about an idea for a cartoon character. Draw it on paper or on a computer. Give your character a name, and write a paragraph to describe him or her.

 Find out more about animation at **www.macmillanmh.com**.

CA **Writing**

✓ **Sensory Details**

Include **sensory details** in your writing that tell about how something looks, feels, smells, tastes, or sounds.

Read the passage below. Notice how author Eileen Christelow uses sensory detail in her story.

An excerpt from
What Do Illustrators Do?

The author writes about the illustrator in the story imagining how the characters will look. She creates a picture of what the illustrator might draw.

Illustrators can use their imaginations or they may have to do some research.

"I'll make Jack look like me in fourth grade."

"What is the shape of the beanstalk leaf?"

"I imagine Jack lives in a small country cottage surrounded by palm trees...."

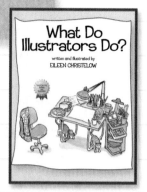

What Do
Illustrators Do?

written and illustrated by
EILEEN CHRISTELOW

Read and Find

Read Justin's writing below. How does he use sensory details to help you picture the moment? Use the tips below to help you.

Soccer Fun

by Justin C.

The cool, crisp air swished over my face. My socks felt soppy from the dew in the grass. I ran to kick the ball to my friend Ryan. The crowds' cheers echoed in my ears, "Go Justin!" Boom! I slammed the ball as hard as I could. It felt like I was kicking a cement wall.

Read about a game of soccer.

Writer's Checklist

✓ Does the writer give you more than just "seeing" details?

✓ Does the writer help you hear, touch, smell, or taste the moment he is describing?

☑ Can you use **sensory details** to imagine how Justin experiences the moment?

My
Art

What story does this art tell you? What are some ways you like to tell stories using your art?

LOG ON ▶ Find out more about expressing yourself in art at **www.macmillanmh.com**.

Vocabulary

annual   politely

potential   wrapping

expensive   innocent

Dictionary

Homophones are words that sound the same but have different meanings and spellings. The words *wrapping* and *rapping* are homophones.

My Winter Vacation

by Meredith Gamel

December 22

We're leaving for Florida to visit Aunt Sue, Uncle Mike, and my cousins Tim and Laura. We go every year over the holidays. I guess you could call this our **annual** trip. The trip has the **potential** for being fun, but I'd rather celebrate at home. Dad's rushing me, so I'd better hurry.

December 23

We're almost there. Last night we stayed at a hotel. Dad said it was **expensive**, but Mom said she didn't care what it cost, she needed a break from being in the car. I got to swim in the hotel pool. It felt good after sitting in the car all day.

December 26

We have been at Aunt Sue's for two days. Yesterday she made lobsters for lunch. They looked terrible—like big, red bugs! I **politely** said, "No, thank you. I'm sticking with tuna!"

Today I found a package covered in brown paper on my bed. It was from Grandma. I took off the **wrapping** paper. It's a wave board! Time to go to the beach and try it out. Yay!

December 28

I love the ocean, but the water is freezing! Laura dumped a pail of water on my dad. Boy, did he jump! She tried to look sweet and **innocent**, but Dad knew she had done it. She does it every year!

December 30

Last day at the beach. I wish we didn't have to go. Anyway, school starts in a few days, and Mom says we need to go grocery shopping. While I'm going up and down the food aisles, I'll think about the beach and look forward to using my wave board again.

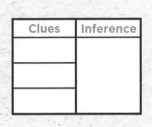

Reread for **Comprehension**

Visualize

Make Inferences Authors do not always tell you every detail in a story. Sometimes you need to use story **clues** and what you already know to make **inferences** about plot or characters. Visualizing, or picturing, what happens in a story can help you make inferences. Reread the selection. Use your Inference Chart to help you make inferences about "My Winter Vacation."

Clues	Inference

Award
Winning
Illustrator

Comprehension

Genre

Realistic Fiction is an invented story that could have happened in real life.

Visualize

Make Inferences
As you read, use your Inference Chart.

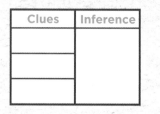

Clues	Inference

Read to Find Out

How will Steven find a present for his aunt?

FAMILY EXPRESS

WRITTEN AND ILLUSTRATED BY JAVAKA STEPTOE

Every summer for as long as I can remember, my Aunt Carolyn has gone traveling. Sometimes she would go out of the country and other times she just got on a train and visited different places. She always had funny stories to tell when she returned.

I thought Aunt Carolyn's stories were so much fun that once, when I was three, I hid in her suitcase so she would take me with her. She was so tickled, she promised to send me a postcard from every place she went until I was old enough to travel with her. Grandma had to read the postcards to me at first, but as I got older, I read them myself.

Those postcards always made me feel special.

> **Make Inferences**
> How does Aunt Carolyn feel about the narrator? How do you know?

This summer Aunt Carolyn said she would be here for our **annual** block party. The block party was my favorite time of the year because the whole family visited us at Grandma's house. People came from everywhere, and there was a lot of food, music, and things to do.

Aunt Carolyn didn't come back often, so I wanted to get something special for her. I just didn't know what.

The night before the party, I barely got any sleep. My cousin Sean was staying over, and I had to share my bed with him. Sean was always asking questions.

"Why do dogs like dog biscuits?" he asked.

"I don't know," I answered, but I wasn't really listening. I just lay there thinking until I came up with an idea. Maybe I could find something for Aunt Carolyn on Nostrand Avenue! You can buy almost anything there.

The next morning I woke up to the smell of Grandma's pancakes.

"Get up, Sean," I said, poking him in his ribs. "It's time to get up!" We got dressed and ran downstairs.

"Good morning, Grandma," we sang as we sat down to heaping plates of her buttery-syrupy pancakes.

Uncle Charles walked in, grumpy as usual. Sean and I covered our plates with our arms because Uncle Charles liked to take bites of your food.

"Stop it, Charles," Grandma said just as he reached for one of my pancakes.

"I only do it out of love," Uncle Charles replied, acting all **innocent**. "I want to make sure it's not poisoned."

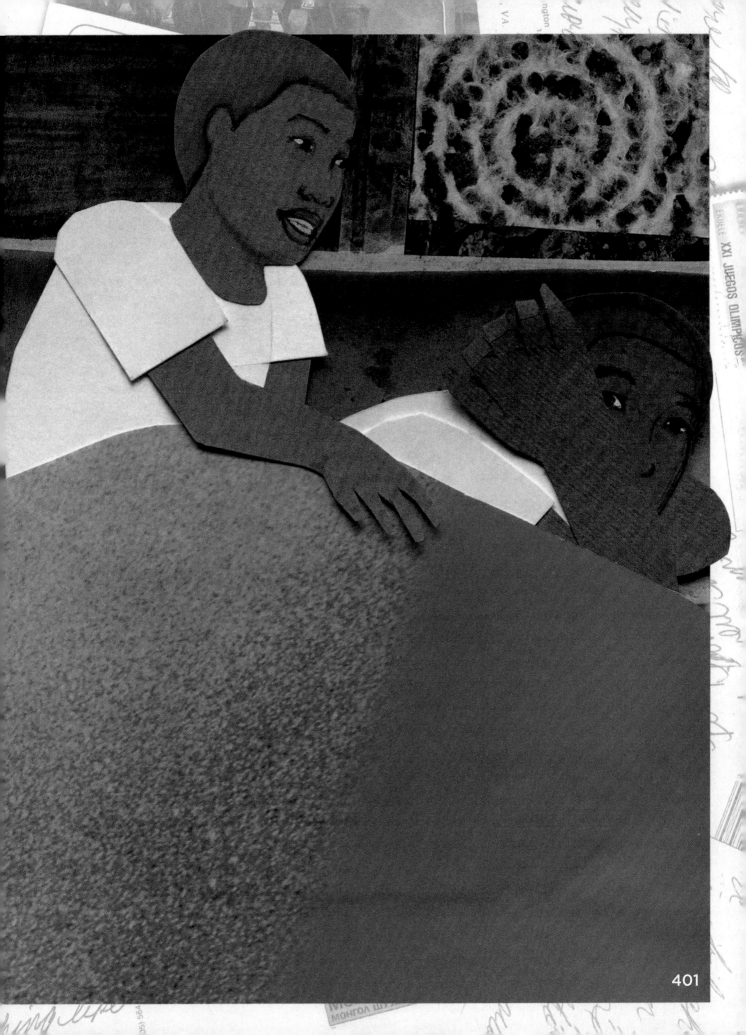

In between bites Sean told Grandma how he'd been working on a rap for the block party talent show.

Suddenly the phone rang.

"Hey, Carolyn," Grandma said in her cheery voice. "When are you getting in?... The 2:30 train? You need anything?... All right then, we'll see you soon."

I looked at my watch. I had only about four and a half hours until Aunt Carolyn arrived!

Just then Aunt Marsha walked in carrying three big bags of potatoes.

I looked at Sean. "We better get out of here before they have us peeling potatoes," I whispered.

When we reached the vestibule door, we heard country music blasting. That could mean only one thing. Granddad! I didn't want to get trapped having to help Granddad make his secret barbecue sauce that everybody knew the secret to. Besides, Granddad liked to tell long stories.

"Sean," I said. "Go talk to Granddad. I'll be out in a minute."

As soon as Sean was gone, I ran up to my room, climbed out the window onto our neighbor's toolshed, and made my way past her garden to the street. Then I headed toward Nostrand Avenue.

The center of Chicago's Grant Park,
Fountain is of the most regularly visited attractions
Chicago.

The first place I went was Perkins Drugstore. The store had shelves and shelves of stuff. I wandered up and down the aisles, picking up things, until I heard someone come up behind me.

"How may I help you, young maaaaan?" I cringed. It was Mr. Perkins, the owner. He had the screechiest voice ever. It was like nails scratching on a chalkboard.

I told him I wanted to find a special gift for my favorite aunt.

"What about some caaards?" Mr. Perkins said. "Or we have delicious chocolaaaates. She might like some perfuuuume."

I shook my head no, so he started suggesting other things. I listened **politely** until my head started to hurt.

"Thank you," I said finally. "Let me think about it some more." Then I walked quickly out of the store, rubbing my ears.

Next I went to Ms. Ruby's shop. She's from Jamaica. She had lots of handmade things in her store, and I loved the way she talked.

"Hey, sweetie. How you do?" Ms. Ruby asked.

"I'm looking for a surprise for my Aunt Carolyn," I answered, looking around the shop. "I've saved up ten dollars and seventy-five cents."

"Okay," Ms. Ruby said. "She must be really special. You see anything you might like?"

"What about that picture frame?" I said. "Aunt Carolyn loves elephants."

"That one kinda **expensive**," she said. "It cost twenty-seven dollars."

I put on my best smile and told her I was a little short.

"You short for true," she said, and chuckled. "If you did have a likkle more money, I woulda sell it to you. But sorry, m'love. The money too short. You see a next one that you like?"

I looked around but didn't see anything else.

"No, thank you," I said. I left Ms. Ruby's feeling a little down.

As I left the store, I saw Uncle Charles walking toward me. I tried to hide, but he had already spotted me.

"Where have you been, Steven?" Uncle Charles asked. "It's almost time for the block party."

Uncle Charles knew how to fix all sorts of things, but he wouldn't do anything unless you paid him. Not even for kids. He was my last chance, though.

"I've been looking for a present for Aunt Carolyn," I explained. "Ms. Ruby's shop is too expensive, and there's nothing special enough at Perkins's."

"Come with me," Uncle Charles said. "I've got just the thing. How much money do you have?"

"Ten dollars," I said. I kept the seventy-five cents for myself. I couldn't let him take all my money!

We went to Uncle Charles's house, which was pretty junky. He had some of everything there—bike parts, old toys, magazines, radios, VCRs, you name it.

Uncle Charles started rummaging around his apartment, looking for things that might be useful. Every few minutes he would hold up something weird.

"What about this?" Uncle Charles would ask.

I would shake my head no.

"You've got to give me some help here," Uncle Charles complained after I said no to several things. So I started digging around. All of a sudden, there it was, the perfect thing.

"Look at this!" I said, holding up a big toy train. It needed a lot of fixing up—the paint was peeling off and some of the windows were broken, but I could see it had **potential**. I got busy right away. I had to work fast if I was going to finish in time to meet Aunt Carolyn at the train station.

I arrived at the station just as the train was coming in. A big crowd of people rushed down the stairs toward me. After almost everybody had left the station, I spotted Aunt Carolyn.

"Hey, Steven!" Aunt Carolyn called. She bustled over and plopped down her bags. She gave me a big kiss, and I gave her a nice, big hug.

"How's my little man doing?" Aunt Carolyn said. "Oh! You've gotten so big and handsome. I don't know who's more handsome now, you or Sean."

"Me of course!" I said, and we both just laughed.

"So what do you have there, Steven?" Aunt Carolyn asked, pointing to the package under my arm.

"It's a surprise for you," I said as I handed her the package.

Without saying a word, Aunt Carolyn opened her gift. As soon as she got the **wrapping** off, she put the train up to her face and turned it around and around.

"Steven," Aunt Carolyn said, and gave a big laugh. "This is the best present anyone has ever given me!"

When we got back to my block, everyone was so excited to see Aunt Carolyn that they didn't ask where I had been. They surrounded her as if she were a movie star, their voices shouting out from every direction.

"How have you been, Carolyn?" someone called.

"What did you bring me?" joked another.

"Were you really in Alaska?" asked Sean.

Instead of answering them, Aunt Carolyn held up the train. "Isn't this the most wonderful thing you've ever seen?" she said.

Eagerly they passed around the train, and everyone took real long, careful looks. Sometimes people laughed or made comments.

"Yeah," said Uncle Charles. "That sure is Grandma, always on the phone."

"Look at the Afros on Uncle Charles and Aunt Marsha!" Grandma said, rolling her eyes.

"The Jones Family Express, that sure is right!" said Granddad, chuckling.

Everyone liked the train, even Sean, who made a face and said I should have chosen a better picture of him.

The rest of the day flew by. Aunt Carolyn put her train on an old cake stand in the kitchen window where everyone could see it.

Granddad cooked his best batch of barbecue ever. There were so many greasy barbecue-stained little kids running around that it looked as if they had been in a mud fight. Sean actually won the rap contest. The band liked him so much, they let him be a special guest DJ until it was time to pack up the music. The most surprising thing of all was that Uncle Charles bought ice cream for everybody with my ten dollars and didn't try to eat anyone else's but his own.

> **Make Inferences**
> Why does Uncle Charles buy ice cream for everyone?

414

Aunt Carolyn sat next to me on the stoop as the whole family told stories, played games, and fought over the last bit of food.

"Steven, thank you for making me feel so special," Aunt Carolyn said. She gave me a little hug and handed me a postcard.

I turned over the postcard and read the message aloud. "Good for one trip with Aunt Carolyn."

I couldn't believe my eyes. I was finally old enough to travel with Aunt Carolyn! Who would have guessed that at the end of the day, I would get the best present of all.

A Postcard from Javaka Steptoe

Javaka Steptoe got the idea for this story from his grandmother. She had an operation and could not go out. Javaka asked a traveling friend to send her postcards from different places to make her feel better. Javaka often uses experiences from his own life in his books. He especially likes to write and illustrate stories about families. He wants readers to open his books and find something that reminds them of their own families.

Other books by Javaka Steptoe: *Hot Day on Abbott Avenue* and *In Daddy's Arms I Am Tall*

 LOG ON ▶ Find out more about Javaka Steptoe at **www.macmillanmh.com**.

CA Author's Purpose

Fiction authors often write to entertain or inform. Why did Javaka Steptoe write this story? What details from *The Jones Family Express* help you figure out his purpose for writing?

(CA) Critical Thinking

Summarize

Summarize *The Jones Family Express.* Use your Inference Chart to help you tell about the characters and their actions.

Clues	Inference

Think and Compare

1. What **inference** can you make about how Steven and Aunt Carolyn feel about each other? What information in the story helps you make this inference? **Visualize: Make Inferences**

2. Reread pages 412–414 of *The Jones Family Express.* What makes Steven's train more special than most toy trains? Use details from both the story and the illustrations in your answer. **Evaluate**

3. Would you enjoy traveling with Aunt Carolyn? Why or why not? **Apply**

4. Why might some people enjoy a handmade present more than an **expensive** store-bought present? **Evaluate**

5. Read "My Winter Vacation" on pages 394–395. How does the journal writer seem to feel about her family? How do her feelings compare with Steven's feelings for his family? Use details from both selections in your answer. **Reading/Writing Across Texts**

Egyptian art from the 16th century B.C. shows us how they decorated their horses and chariots.

From Here to There

by Lauren Eckler

How do you get from here to there? Cars, trains, and planes help you to travel fairly quickly and easily. But transportation has not always been easy.

Walking and Riding

People have lived on Earth for millions of years. For much of that time, there was only one way of getting around: walking. Think of how different our lives would be if we had to walk everywhere!

Luckily, inventions in transportation made it easier to travel. Roman soldiers built thousands of miles of roads throughout Europe. People walked or rode animals on these roads. Then, they built carts and wagons pulled by horses to use on the roads. They also used maps to find their way. Early Chinese **civilizations** built roads and boats, too. They even set speed limits on their roads 3,000 years ago!

Water, Water, Everywhere

Egyptians made sailboats 5,000 years ago. Boats helped ancient peoples cross large bodies of water. This allowed cultures to meet, trade with each other, and explore new lands.

Bigger, Better, Faster

Our **ancestors** would be proud to see that we still use many of their inventions, such as maps. People in the future will still be looking for better ways to get from here to there.

Using a Map
Reading Directions

Suppose you were a traveler long ago. You would need a map to plan your route. Use the following set of directions to help you read the map:

1. Find where you want to go.

2. Find your current position.

3. Plan a route. Highlight the route on your map.

4. Pay attention to symbols on the map. Look at the compass rose and the map key.

 Critical Thinking

1. Why must you do Steps 1 and 2 before Step 3? **Reading Directions**

2. How did the invention of roads and boats change the lives of the ancient cultures? **Make Inferences**

3. What type of transportation is mentioned in *The Jones Family Express*? How would that story be different if it took place in ancient times? **Reading/Writing Across Texts**

 History/Social Science Activity

Research a type of transportation. Take a survey of students who have been in or on your topic. Show your results in a graph.

LOG ON ▶ Find out more about transportation at **www.macmillanmh.com**.

Reading and Writing Connection

Sensory Details

Using **sensory details** in your writing helps your reader to see a more detailed picture.

Read the passage below. Notice how author Javaka Steptoe uses sensory detail in his story.

An excerpt from
The Jones Family Express

The author uses sensory details to help us do more than just "see" this moment. The author chooses details about what Steven and Sean smell, feel, and taste to help us imagine their morning very clearly.

The next morning I woke up to the smell of Grandma's pancakes.

"Get up, Sean," I said, poking him in his ribs. "It's time to get up!" We got dressed and ran downstairs.

"Good morning, Grandma," we sang as we sat down to heaping plates of her buttery-syrupy pancakes.

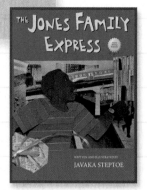

THE JONES FAMILY EXPRESS

WRITTEN AND ILLUSTRATED BY
JAVAKA STEPTOE

Read and Find

Read Arielle's writing below. How does she use sensory details to help you imagine the moment? Use the tips below to help you.

A Wild Ride
by Arielle G.

I get goosebumps on my arms while I wait in line for the waterslide. The metal steps are cold but I don't mind. I grip the slippery rails tightly. At the top of the slide, I push off and feel the hot plastic under my legs. Splash! When I land in the water, it goes up my nose and all I can smell and taste are pool chemicals.

Read about my ride on the waterslide.

Writer's Checklist

✓ Does the writer give you more than just "seeing" details?

✓ Does the writer help you hear, touch, smell, or taste the moment she is describing?

☑ What **sensory details** help you imagine how Arielle experiences the moment?

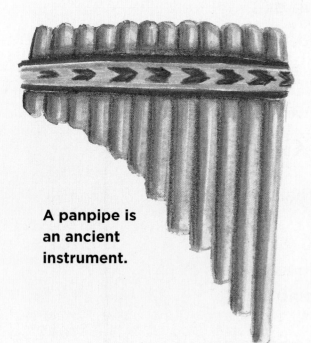

Review

Sequence
Draw Conclusions
Main Idea and Details
Homophones
Directions

Felicia's Choice

A panpipe is an ancient instrument.

Felicia loved music. On Felicia's eighth birthday, her mother said to her, "I think you're ready to choose an instrument to play."

Felicia wanted very much to learn to play her own instrument, but she couldn't make up her mind. She loved the sounds that each instrument made. First, she thought she wanted to play the piano. The next day, she wanted to play the guitar. The day after that, she wanted to play drums.

A week later, Felicia's mom said, "Let's go to the Music Center. We can hear a symphony orchestra. I think that you will love it. Plus, it might help you pick your instrument."

Felicia was excited. After they got off the bus, they took a cab to the concert hall. There they listened to one of the best orchestras in the world. Felicia nearly cried because the music was so lovely. There was only one problem. Felicia still could not make up her mind about an instrument. First, she wanted to play the flute. Then, she wanted to play the trumpet. By the third piece, she wanted to play the clarinet. They all sounded so beautiful.

After the concert, Felicia's mom said, "Let's go to dinner. I know a great restaurant nearby."

They walked down Main Street At the next corner, Felicia heard something wonderful. "Mom!" she cried, "Let's go see who's making that music!"

They walked around the corner. There they saw a group of musicians from Peru. Each member was playing an instrument that Felicia had never seen before. It was made of wooden tubes, side by side in a raft shape. Each tube was a different length. Felicia asked the musicians, "What are these called?"

"In Peru, we call them siku," said one musician. "Here, people call them panpipes."

"Mom, I finally made up my mind. I know what I want to play!" exclaimed Felicia.

Design Your Own Journal

Journal writing can be fun. You can write journal entries about important things or interesting experiences. No matter what you write, your journal will be filled with memories.

Here are some directions for making your own journal. Follow the steps in order. Soon you'll have a journal that is made by you and tells all about you.

What You'll Need

- sheets of white or colored paper
- two pieces of thin cardboard
- ruler, scissors, glue
- binder clips, stapler
- colored markers, paints, and pens
- decorations, such as yarn, stickers, photos

Make Your Journal Covers

1. Place a sheet of paper on each piece of cardboard.
2. With a pencil, trace straight lines around each paper's edge.
3. Cut along the lines. These pieces of cardboard will become the covers of your journal.

Bind Your Journal

4. With a pencil, draw a faint, vertical line along the left edge of the cover.

5. Stack the paper for the journal pages between the two cardboard covers. Use binder clips to hold the papers together neatly.

6. With an adult's help, staple along the pencil line. This will hold your journal together.

Decorate Your Journal

7. Now it's time to be creative! Decorate the front and back covers of your journal. Use markers, crayons, paints, or colored pencils to add pictures or words to your covers. You could also glue on shells, yarn, stickers, or photos. Choose decorations that are special to you. Now your journal is ready. Write your first entry.

CA Critical Thinking

Now answer numbers 1 through 4. Base your answers on the passage "Felicia's Choice."

1. **What happens FIRST in the passage?**

   A   Felicia hears musicians from Peru.
   B   Felicia and her mother go to Chinatown.
   C   Felicia's mother says that she can choose an instrument to learn.
   D   Felicia and her mother go to a concert hall.

2. **Which word BEST describes Felicia in this passage?**

   A   weak
   B   lonely
   C   courageous
   D   indecisive

3. **Read this sentence from the passage.**

> "We can hear a symphony orchestra. I think you will love it."

   Which of the following words from these sentences could be spelled differently and have a different meaning?

   A   think
   B   hear
   C   orchestra
   D   love

4. **Describe the events that happen on the day Felicia finally chooses an instrument. What happens first, second, and last? Use details from the passage to support your answer.**

428

Now answer numbers 1 through 4. Base your answers on the article "Design Your Own Journal."

1. **What is the FIRST thing to do when you make a journal?**

A   Cut the cardboard.

B   Trace around the paper's edge.

C   Put paper on cardboard.

D   Glue decorations onto your cover.

2. **What is the MAIN IDEA of this article?**

A   You can make your own journal.

B   Everyone should keep a journal.

C   Journals help us decide what we think.

D   It's difficult to make a journal.

3. **Which of these should you ask an adult to help you with?**

A   tracing straight lines

B   coloring your cover

C   stapling your journal together

D   choosing decorations

4. **When making a journal, what should you do LAST?**

A   Stack papers.

B   Trace a line on the cover.

C   Decorate the cover.

D   Cut cardboard to make covers.

Write on Demand

PROMPT People write stories, plays, and poems and draw pictures in journals. What would you write in a journal? Use details from the article to support your answer. Write for 8 minutes. Write as much as you can, as well as you can.

Glossary

What Is a Glossary?

A glossary can help you find the **meanings** of words in this book that you may not know. The words in the glossary are listed in **alphabetical order**. **Guide words** at the top of each page tell you the first and last words on the page.

Each word is divided into syllables. The way to pronounce the word is given next. You can understand the pronunciation respelling by using the **pronunciation key** at the right. A shorter key appears at the bottom of every other page. When a word has more than one syllable, a dark accent mark (´) shows which syllable is stressed. In some words, a light accent mark (´) shows which syllable has a less heavy stress. Sometimes an entry includes a second meaning for the word.

potential

equipment

Guide Words

First word on the page   Last word on the page

Sample Entry

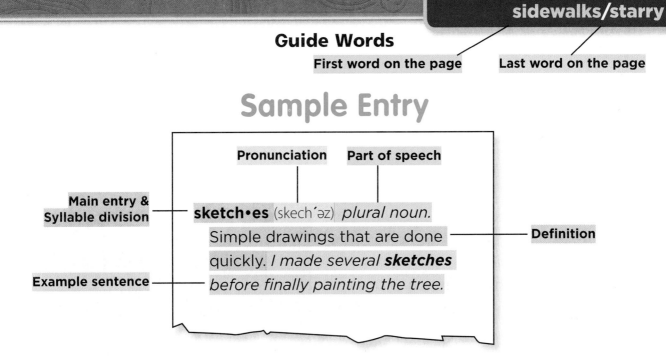

Pronunciation   Part of speech

Main entry & Syllable division

sketch•es (skech′əz) *plural noun.*
Simple drawings that are done quickly. *I made several **sketches** before finally painting the tree.*

Definition

Example sentence

Pronunciation Key

Phonetic Spelling	Examples
a	**a**t, b**a**d, pl**ai**d, l**au**gh
ā	**a**pe, p**ai**n, d**a**y, br**ea**k
ä	f**a**ther, c**a**lm
âr	**c**are, p**air**, b**ear**, th**eir**, wh**ere**
e	**e**nd, p**e**t, s**ai**d, h**ea**ven, fri**e**nd
ē	**e**qual, m**e**, f**ee**t, t**ea**m, p**ie**ce, k**e**y
i	**i**t, b**i**g, g**i**ve, h**y**mn
ī	**i**ce, f**i**ne, l**ie**, m**y**
îr	**ear**, d**eer**, h**ere**, p**ier**ce
o	**o**dd, h**o**t, w**a**tch
ō	**o**ld, **oa**t, t**oe**, l**ow**
ô	c**o**ffee, **a**ll, t**au**ght, l**aw**, f**ou**ght
ôr	**or**der, f**or**k, h**or**se, st**o**ry, p**our**
oi	**oi**l, t**oy**
ou	**ou**t, n**ow**, b**ou**gh
u	**u**p, m**u**d, l**o**ve, d**ou**ble
ū	**u**se, m**u**le, c**u**e, f**eu**d, f**ew**
ü	r**u**le, tr**u**e, f**oo**d, fr**ui**t
u̇	p**u**t, w**oo**d, sh**ou**ld, l**oo**k
ûr	b**ur**n, h**ur**ry, t**er**m, b**ir**d, w**or**d, c**ou**rage
ə	**a**bout, tak**e**n, penc**i**l, lem**o**n, circ**u**s
b	**b**at, a**b**ove, jo**b**
ch	**ch**in, su**ch**, ma**tch**

Phonetic Spelling	Examples
d	**d**ear, so**d**a, ba**d**
f	**f**ive, de**f**end, lea**f**, o**ff**, cou**gh**, ele**ph**ant
g	**g**ame, a**g**o, fo**g**, e**gg**
h	**h**at, a**h**ead
hw	**wh**ite, **wh**ether, **wh**ich
j	**j**oke, en**j**oy, **g**em, pa**g**e, e**dge**
k	**k**ite, ba**k**ery, see**k**, ta**ck**, **c**at
l	**l**id, sai**l**or, fee**l**, ba**ll**, a**ll**ow
m	**m**an, fa**m**ily, drea**m**
n	**n**ot, fi**n**al, pa**n**, **kn**ife, **gn**aw
ng	lo**ng**, si**ng**er
p	**p**ail, re**p**air, soa**p**, ha**pp**y
r	**r**ide, pa**r**ent, wea**r**, mo**r**e, ma**rr**y
s	**s**it, a**s**ide, pet**s**, **c**ent, pa**ss**
sh	**sh**oe, wa**sh**er, fi**sh**, mi**ss**ion, na**ti**on
t	**t**ag, pre**t**end, fa**t**, dress**ed**
th	**th**in, pan**th**er, bo**th**
<u>th</u>	**<u>th</u>**ese, mo**<u>th</u>**er, smoo**<u>th</u>**
v	**v**ery, fa**v**or, wa**v**e
w	**w**et, **w**eather, re**w**ard
y	**y**es, oni**o**n
z	**z**oo, la**z**y, ja**zz**, ro**s**e, dog**s**, hou**s**es
zh	vi**s**ion, trea**s**ure, sei**z**ure

Aa

ac•cept•ance (ak sep′təns) *noun.* An agreement to take something given or offered. *My sister learned of her **acceptance** to college yesterday.*

ached (ākt) *verb.* To have had a dull and steady pain. *Hannah's tooth **ached** all day, so she went to the dentist.*

ad•mire (ad mīr′) *verb.* To respect or think well of someone or something. *The team had to **admire** the coach for never giving up.*

ad•ven•ture (ad ven′chər) *noun.* An exciting, unusual, or risky experience. *Lisa and her mom went on a camping **adventure** this past summer.*

Word History

Adventure comes from Latin *adventura*, meaning "a thing about to happen."

an•ces•tors (an′ses tərz) *plural noun.* People who lived before you in your family. *Jorge's **ancestors** once lived in an old castle in Spain.*

an•i•ma•tors (an′ə mā′tərz) *plural noun.* Artists or technicians who draw and produce cartoons. *Many **animators** today use computers to bring their drawings to life.*

an•nounced (ə nounst′) *verb.* Told something in a loud or official way. *The winners of the writing contest were **announced** at the assembly.*

an•nu•al (an′ū əl) *adjective.* Happening once a year. *Every July 4, my family holds an **annual** family reunion.*

ap•pli•ances (ə plī′əns əz) *plural noun.* Small machines or devices that have particular uses, such as toasters, refrigerators, and washing machines. *The store was crowded because of the sale on kitchen **appliances**.*

au•di•tions (ô dish′ənz) *plural noun.* Trial performances. *The actor had three **auditions** before being rewarded with the part.*

Bb

batch•es (bach´əz) *plural noun.* Groups of things prepared or gathered together. *Tracey and Darryl made several **batches** of cookies for the bake sale at the library.*

blos•somed (blos´əmd) *verb.* Grew or developed. *The student kept practicing until she **blossomed** into a wonderful violinist.*

both•er•ing (both´ər ing) *verb.* 1. Giving people trouble or annoying them. 2. Taking the time to do something. *1. Henry's need to talk while watching TV was **bothering** Maria. 2. My dad said no without even **bothering** to look up from the paper.*

busi•ness (biz´nis) *noun.* 1. The work a person does to earn a living. 2. The buying and selling of things; trade. *1. Kenneth worked in the fashion **business** for eight years. 2. The kite shop does good **business** in the summer.*

Cc

cap•ture (kap´chər) *verb.* To catch and hold a person, animal, or thing. *The park rangers were trying to **capture** the bear that was roaming the picnic area.*

chuck•led (chuk´əld) *verb.* Laughed in a quiet way. *When the plan worked, Calvin **chuckled** to himself.*

cit•i•zen (sit´ə zən) *noun.* A person who lives in a community and has rights and duties. *Each **citizen** in our town has the right to vote for a mayor.*

civ•i•li•za•tions (siv´ə lə zā´shənz) *plural noun.* Groups of people sharing a way of life in a specific place or time. *Historians study ancient **civilizations** to learn how people lived in the past.*

---

at; āpe; fär; câre; end; mē; it; īce; pîerce; hot; ōld; sông; fôrk; oil; out; up; ūse; rüle; pùll; tûrn; chin; sing; shop; thin; **th**is; hw in white; zh in treasure.

The symbol ə stands for the unstressed vowel sound in about, taken, pencil, lemon, and circus.

com•mu•ni•cate (kə mū′ni kāt′) *verb.* To pass along or exchange information, thoughts, or ideas. *It is difficult to* **communicate** *with people who do not listen.*

com•mu•ni•ty (kə mū′ni tē) *noun, pl.* **com•mu•ni•ties.** 1. A group of people who live together in the same place. 2. A group of people who share a common interest. *1. Our* **community** *voted to build a new library. 2. The scientific* **community** *is involved in important research projects.*

con•cen•trate (kon′sən trāt′) *verb.* To pay attention or think very carefully about something being done. *If the radio is on, I find it hard to* **concentrate** *on anything else.*

con•struc•tion (kə n struk′shən) *noun.* The act or process of building something. *It was interesting to watch the* **construction** *of our town's new grocery store.*

con•trib•ute (kən trib′yūt) *verb.* To give, or supply along with others. *The club organizers asked members to* **contribute** *several hours of their time, to help with the special event.*

crack•le (krak′əl) *verb.* To make a series of small, sharp snapping noises. *I like to hear the burning wood* **crackle** *in the fireplace.*

cul•ture (kul′chər) *noun.* Characteristics, beliefs, and behaviors of a social group. *The travelers were excited to experience the country's* **culture**.

Dd

de•mand (di mand′) *noun.* An urgent requirement or need. *Katie knew there was a* **demand** *for blankets at the dog shelter.*

den (den) *noun.* 1. A place, often underground or in a cave, where wild animals live. 2. A small, cozy room for reading or studying. *1. The bears crawl into their* **den** *each winter for a long sleep. 2. Jane studies at her computer in the* **den**.

de•serve (di zûrv´) *verb.* To have a right to something. *I believe I **deserve** to be on the soccer team because I practiced after school and on weekends.*

de•ter•mi•na•tion (di tûr´mə nā´shən) *noun.* A firm purpose. *Miguel's **determination** made him study very hard to get the best test score in the class.*

dis•ap•pear (dis´ə pîr´) *verb.* To stop existing or become extinct. *Elephants began to **disappear** because so many people hunted them for their tusks.*

do•nate (dō´nāt´) *verb.* To give or offer. *Every winter my family will **donate** winter clothes we no longer wear.*

Ee

en•clo•sure (en klō´zhər) *noun.* A place that is surrounded by a fence or wall on all sides. *The animals were kept in an **enclosure** until their owners came to pick them up.*

e•quip•ment (i kwip´mənt) *noun.* Anything that is provided for a special purpose or use. *The firefighters showed the class all the different **equipment** they have and how it is used.*

es•tab•lished (i stab´lishd) *verb.* To have set up permanently. *The colony was **established** in 1734.*

es•ti•mate (es´ tə māt´) *verb.* To approximate. *Greg asked the sailmaker to **estimate** the amount of canvas that would be needed to sew a new sail.*

ex•act (eg zakt´) *adjective.* Very accurate. *I need to know the **exact** time because I can't be one minute late.*

---

at; āpe; fär; câre; end; mē; it; īce; pîerce; hot; ōld; sông; fôrk; oil; out; up; ūse; rüle; pull; tûrn; chin; sing; shop; thin; this; hw in white; zh in treasure.

The symbol ə stands for the unstressed vowel sound in about, taken, pencil, lemon, and circus.

ex•cite•ment (ek sīt′mənt) *noun.* A feeling of being happy because something good has happened or will happen. *The class was full of* **excitement** *before the show began.*

ex•pen•sive (ek spen′siv) *adjective.* Costing a lot of money. *A wonderful gift does not have to be* **expensive**.

ex•plor•ing (ik splôr′ing) *verb.* Searching for purpose of discovery. *Amy has been* **exploring** *her new neighborhood since her family moved.*

Ff

fan•tas•tic (fan tas′tik) *adjective.* 1. Very unusual. 2. Splendid. *1. The artist's favorite drawings were of mythical and* **fantastic** *animals. 2. Emily's flute playing was* **fantastic**.

fo•cus (fō′kəs) *verb.* 1. An adjustment to produce a clear image. 2. A point of attention. *1. A good photographer will always* **focus** *carefully before snapping the picture. 2. My coach always reminds me to* **focus** *on the ball before swinging.*

form (fôrm) *noun.* 1. A body or figure. 2. The state in which something exists. 3. A document that requires information to be added. *1. Although it was foggy, the* **form** *of a tall figure could be seen. 2. Jello is meant to be eaten in its solid* **form**, *not liquid. 3. Before the dentist would see me, I had to fill in a* **form**.

fum•bled (fum′bəld) *verb.* Tried to get hold of or handled in a clumsy way. *I* **fumbled** *around in the dark for my glasses.*

func•tion (fungk′shən) *noun.* The proper action or purpose of something. *The **function** of the heart is to pump blood through the body.*

Gg

ge•o•met•ric (jē′ə met′rik) *adjective.* 1. Of or relating to geometry. 2. Made up or decorated with lines, angles, triangles. *1. The triangle is a **geometric** form. 2. The rug had **geometric** patterns.*

Word History

Geometric is a combination of *ge* "earth, land" and *metria,* from Greek *metrein,* "to measure."

grum•bled (grum′bəld) *verb.* Complained in a low voice. *The class **grumbled** when the teacher gave them a lot of homework to do over the holiday.*

Hh

harm•ing (här′ming) *verb.* Doing damage to or hurting. *The construction company was told that it was **harming** the environment, because it cut down so many trees.*

Ii

il•lus•trate (il′ə strāt′) *verb.* To draw a picture or diagram; to explain or decorate something written. *The art teacher helped me **illustrate** my story.*

at; āpe; fär; câre; end; mē; it; īce; pîerce; hot; ōld; sông; fôrk; oil; out; up; ūse; rüle; pu̇ll; tûrn; chin; sing; shop; thin; <u>th</u>is; hw in white; zh in treasure.

The symbol ə stands for the unstressed vowel sound in about, taken, pencil, lemon, and circus.

im•ages (im´ ij æz) *plural noun.* Pictures of persons or things. *I still have **images** in my head of the beautiful sunset at the beach.*

Word History

Image comes from the Latin *imago,* or *imitari,* "to imitate."

im•mi•grants (im´ i grənts) *plural noun.* People who move from one country to live in another. *Most **immigrants** to the United States passed through Ellis Island.*

im•proved (im prüvd´) *verb.* Made or became better. *Her singing ability has greatly **improved** since last year.*

Word History

Improve is from the Middle English *improwen,* "to enclose land for farming," and from Anglo-Norman *emprouwer,* "to turn to profit."

in•flu•enced (in´ flü ənsd) *verb.* Changed or affected behavior or thought. *Sam **influenced** his sister to read the same comic book.*

in•no•cent (in´ə sənt) *adjective.* Not guilty; harmless. *The puppy looked **innocent**, but we knew she knocked over the cup.*

in•stance (in´ stəns) *noun.* An occurance. *The witness recalled an **instance** when the door was left unlocked.*

Ll

laws (lôz) *plural noun.* Sets of rules that tell people in a community how to behave. *Drivers must obey certain safety **laws**.*

leak•y (lē´kē) *adjective.* Having a hole or small opening that water, light, or air can pass through. *The **leaky** hose caused a big puddle whenever I tried to water the plants.*

lone•some (lōn′səm) *adjective.* Not often visited by people; deserted. *The **lonesome** house in the swamp was a sad sight.*

luck•i•est (luk′ē est) *adjective.* Having or bringing the most good luck. *Of all the contest winners, James was the **luckiest**; he won the grand prize.*

Mm

mem•bers (mem′bərz) *plural noun.* Persons, animals, or things belonging to a group. *The **members** of the basketball team met at the park every Thursday to practice.*

Nn

na•tion (nā′shən) *noun.* A group of people who live in one land and share the same government, laws, and language. *Our **nation** celebrates a national holiday on July 4.*

need•y (nē′dē) *adjective.* Being in a position of want. *My family adopted the **needy** kitten that appeared on our door step.*

nerv•ous (nûr′vəs) *adjective.* Not able to relax; tense or fearful. *Barking dogs make my aunt **nervous**.*

Word History

Nervous comes from the Latin word *nervosus*, meaning "sinewy" or "containing nerves."

non•sense (non′sens) *noun.* Words or actions that are silly and make no sense. *The talk about a monster in the closet was **nonsense**.*

at; āpe; fär; câre; end; mē; it; īce; pîerce; hot; ōld; sông; fôrk; oil; out; up; ūse; rüle; pu̇ll; tûrn; chin; sing; shop; thin; this; hw in white; zh in treasure.

The symbol ə stands for the unstressed vowel sound in about, taken, pencil, lemon, and circus.

no•ticed (nō′tisd) *verb.* Became aware of. *Keith was not* **noticed** *until he raised his hand to ask the question.*

Oo

off•spring (ôf′spring′) *plural noun.* The young of a person, animal, or plant. *A lioness and her three* **offspring** *approached the water hole, frightening off the other animals.*

or•gan•i•za•tion (ôr′gən i zā′shən) *noun.* A group of persons united for a particular purpose. *Katheryn joined that* **organization** *because she believed in their goal for a cleaner environment.*

own•ers (ō′nərz) *plural noun.* People who possess something. *The* **owners** *of the new store put out a sign to advertise.*

Pp

pas•sion (pash′ən) *noun.* A very strong feeling or liking for something. *Love is a* **passion**, *and so is anger.*

po•lite•ly (pə līt′lē) *adverb.* In a way that shows good manners or consideration for others' feelings. *When my friend arrived, he greeted my parents* **politely**.

po•ten•tial (pə ten′shəl) *noun.* The possibility to become something more. *The runners had great* **potential**, *but they would have to practice more.*

pre•served (pri zûrvd′) *verb.* Protected from harm. *Mr. Smith built a fence around the sapling so it would be* **preserved**.

proj•ect (proj′ekt′) *noun.* A plan or proposal. *The class* **project** *took several weeks to complete.*

prop•er (prop′ər) *adjective.* Correct or suitable for a certain purpose. *My brother showed me the* **proper** *way to tie a necktie.*

pro•tect (prə tekt′) *verb.* To defend from harm. *Mr. Trang used an umbrella to* **protect** *himself from the rain.*

Rr

re•cord[1] (ri kôrd´) *verb.* To preserve. *The audio technician prepared to **record** the musician's new song.*

re•cord[2] (re kərd´) *noun.* An account preserved. *The accountant kept a **record** of the company's transactions.*

rent (rent) *1. noun. 2. verb.* 1. Payment for the use of property. 2. To lease. *1. Henry and Mike split the **rent** evenly. 2. When we go on vacation this year, we will **rent** a cabin rather than stay in a hotel.*

rep•u•ta•tion (rep´yə tā´shən) *noun.* What most people think of a person or thing. *Micheline's **reputation** as a speller has gotten better since she won the spelling bee.*

ru•ined (rü´ind) *verb.* Damaged greatly or harmed. *The flood **ruined** all our carpets in the basement.*

Ss

script (skript) *noun.* 1. The text of a play, movie, or television show. 2. A style of writing using cursive characters. *1. The **script** wasn't very long, so it would be easy for her to memorize the lines. 2. The boy had not learned how to write **script**, so he printed the words instead.*

Word History

Script comes from Latin *scribere*, meaning "to write."

sep•a•rate (sep´ə rāt´) *verb.* To set apart or place apart. *After the big fight, we had to **separate** the cat and the dog and put them in different rooms.*

ser•vi•ces (sûr´vis əz) *plural noun.* A variety of tasks or acts done for others, usually for pay. *The car wash provided other **services**, such as dusting and vacuuming inside the car.*

---

at; āpe; fär; câre; end; mē; it; īce; pîerce; hot; ōld; sông; fôrk; oil; out; up; ūse; rüle; půll; tûrn; chin; sing; shop; thin; **th**is; hw in white; zh in treasure.

The symbol ə stands for the unstressed vowel sound in about, taken, pencil, lemon, and circus.

side•walks (sīd′wôks) *plural noun.* Paths by the side of the street or road, usually made of cement. *Vladimir and Bill were paid to shovel snow off the **sidewalks** around their apartment building.*

sin•gle (sing′gəl) *adjective.* One. *Not a **single** person knew about the event.*

sketch•es (skech′əz) *plural noun.* Simple drawings that are done quickly. *I made several **sketches** before finally painting the tree.*

slo•gan (slō′gən) *noun.* A phrase, statement, or motto. *Today our teacher asked us to think up a **slogan** for our science club.*

soared (sôrd) *verb.* Flew high in the air. *The hawk **soared** above the meadow.*

spar•kling (spär′kəl ing) *verb.* Shining or giving off sparks. *The water was **sparkling** in the sunlight.*

splen•did (splen′did) *adjective.* Very good or beautiful. *Some birds have **splendid** feathers of many colors.*

Word History

The word splendid comes from the Latin *splendere*, "to shine."

star•ry (stär′ē) *adjective.* Full of stars or heavenly bodies that shine by their own light. *The **starry** sky made the nighttime seem bright.*

stor•age (stôr′ij) *noun.* A place for keeping things for future use. *Mr. Chen used his garage mainly for* **storage***.*

sto•ry•board (stôr′ē bôrd′) *noun.* A series of drawings or sketches that shows how the action of a film or video will be shot. *According to the* **storyboard***, there would be a lot of special effects in the next scene.*

style (stīl) *noun.* A particular way of saying or doing something. *Every singer has his or her own* **style***.*

Word History

A long time ago, the word **style** meant "a pen," which came from the Latin *stylus,* "a pointed instrument used for writing."

suc•cess (sək ses′) *noun.* A favorable achievement. *The rocket launch was a complete* **success***.*

sug•ges•tions (səg jes′chənz) *plural noun.* Ideas or plans offered for others to think about. *The artist made* **suggestions** *for ways to improve Arthur's painting.*

sup•ply (sə plī′) *noun.* An amount of something needed or available for use. *We had a* **supply** *of candles and batteries in the closet in case of an emergency.*

Tt

tal•ent•ed (tal′ən tid) *adjective.* Having a natural ability or skill. *I didn't know Curtis was such a* **talented** *pianist.*

tech•nol•o•gy (tek nol′ə jē) *noun.* 1. The use of science for practical purposes, especially in engineering and industry. 2. Methods, machines, and devices that are used in doing things in a science or profession. *1. Medical* **technology** *has helped doctors to diagnose illnesses. 2. The artist used new* **technology** *to improve her computer graphics.*

at; āpe; fär; câre; end; mē; it; īce; pîerce; hot; ōld; sông; fôrk; oil; out; up; ūse; rüle; pùll; tûrn; chin; sing; shop; thin; this; hw in white; zh in treasure.

The symbol ə stands for the unstressed vowel sound in about, taken, pencil, lemon, and circus.

tex•tures (teks´chərz) *plural noun.* The way a surface looks or how it feels when you touch it. *Fabrics have many* **textures**, *from silky to rough.*

3-D (thrē´dē´) *adjective.* Three-dimensional. *The images on the computer created the illusion of being* **3-D**.

thrilled (thrild) *verb.* Filled with pleasure or excitement. *The team members were* **thrilled** *when they heard they had won the championship.*

tour (tôr) *noun.* A trip or journey in which many places are visited or many things are seen. *The guide led a* **tour** *through the museum and explained all the famous artwork.*

trad•ers (trā´dərz) *plural noun.* People who buy and sell things as a business. *The* **traders** *went to the settlers to sell them blankets and clothes.*

tra•di•tion•al (trə dish´ə nəl) *adjective.* Coming from established customs. *On holidays, it is* **traditional** *for the Lee family to wear nice clothing at dinner.*

trudged (trujd) *verb.* Walked slowly and with effort. *The children* **trudged** *up the snowy hill to go sledding.*

Uu

un•a•ware (un´ə wâr´) *adjective.* Not conscious of. *The bird was* **unaware** *of the cat watching it.*

use•ful (ūs´fəl) *adjective.* Helpful; serving a good use or purpose. *My mom always tells me to make myself* **useful** *by helping others.*

Vv

vol•un•teers (vol´ən tîrz´) *plural noun.* People who offer to do things by choice and often without pay. *Several* **volunteers** *showed up to help clean up the park and paint the fence.*

Ww

wailed (wāld) *verb.* Made a long and sad cry, especially to show grief or pain. *The baby **wailed** when she dropped her toy.*

wrap•ping (rap′ing) *noun.* Paper or other material used to cover or protect something. *Aunt Marie likes to see pretty **wrapping** on a present.*

at; āpe; fär; câre; end; mē; it; īce; pîerce; hot; ōld; sông; fôrk; oil; out; up; ūse; rüle; pull; tûrn; chin; sing; shop; thin; this; hw in white; zh in treasure.

The symbol ə stands for the unstressed vowel sound in about, taken, pencil, lemon, and circus.

Acknowledgments

The publisher gratefully acknowledges permission to reprint the following copyrighted material:

"Amazing Grace" by Mary Hoffman, illustrations by Caroline Binch. Text copyright © 1991 by Mary Hoffman. Illustrations copyright © 1991 by Caroline Binch. Reprinted by permission of Dial Books for Young Readers, a division of Penguin Young Readers Group.

"Author: A True Story" by Helen Lester. Copyright © 1997 by Helen Lester. Reprinted by permission of Houghton Mifflin Books.

"Boom Town" by Sonia Levitin, illustrations by Cat Bowman Smith. Text copyright © 1998 by Sonia Levitin. Illustrations copyright © 1998 by Cat Bowman Smith. Reprinted with permission by Orchard Books a Grolier Company.

"A Castle on Viola Street" by DyAnne DiSalvo. Copyright © 2001 by DyAnne DiSalvo. Reprinted with permission of HarperCollins Children's Books, a division of HarperCollins Publishers.

"The Caterpillar" by Christina Rossetti from BOOK OF POEMS by Tomie dePaola. Text copyright © 1988 by Tomie dePaola. Reprinted with permission.

"A Child's Call to Aid the Zoo" by Jim Davis. Copyright © 2003 by Jim Davis. Reprinted with permission by The Fresno Bee, a division of the The McClatchy Company.

"Dear Juno" by Soyung Pak, illustrations by Susan Kathleen Hartung. Text copyright © 1999 by Soyung Pak. Illustrations copyright © 1999 by Susan Kathleen Hartung. Reprinted with permission of Penguin Putnam Books for Young Readers, Penguin Books Ltd.

"First Day Jitters" by Julie Danneberg, illustrations by Judy Love. Text copyright © 2000 by Julie Danneberg. Illustrations copyright © 2000 by Judy Love. Reprinted with permission of Charlesbridge, Charlesbridge Publishing, Inc. All rights reserved.

"Home-Grown Butterflies" by Deborah Churchman from RANGER RICK®. Copyright © 1998 by National Wildlife Federation. Reprinted with permission of the National Wildlife Federation, May 1998.

"The Jones Family Express" by Javaka Steptoe. Text and illustrations copyright © 2003 by Javaka Steptoe. Reprinted by permission of Lee & Low Books, Inc.

"Listen" is from A RUMPUS OF RHYMES: A BOOK OF NOISY POEMS is by Bobbi Katz and illustrated by Suan Estelle Kwas. Text copyright © 2001 by Bobby Katz. Illustrations copyright © 2001 by Susan Estell Kwas. Printed by permission of Dutton Children's Books, a division of Penguin Putnam Books for Young Readers.

"Monarch Butterfly" by Marilyn Singer from FIREFLIES AT MIDNIGHT by Marilyn Singer. Text copyright © 2003 by Marilyn Singer. Reprinted with permission by Atheneum Books for Young Readers, an imprint of Simon & Schuster Children's Publishing Division.

"My Very Own Room" by Amada Irma Pérez, illustrations by Maya Christina Gonzalez. Text copyright © 2000 by Amada Irma Pérez. Illustrations copyright © 2000 by Maya Christina Gonzalez. Reprinted with permission by Children's Book Press.

"The Storytelling Stone" is from KEEPERS OF THE EARTH: NATIVE AMERICAN STORIES AND ENVIRONMENTAL ACTIVITIES FOR CHILDREN by Joseph Bruchac. Copyright © 1989 by Joseph Bruchac. Reprinted by permission of Fulcrum Press.

"What Do Illustrators Do?" by Eileen Christelow. Copyright © 1999 by Eileen Christelow. Reprinted with permission by Clarion Books, an imprint of Houghton Mifflin Company.

"Wolf!" by Becky Bloom, illustrations by Pascal Biet. Copyright © 1999 by Siphano, Montpellier. Reprinted with permission by Orchard Books, a Grolier Company.

ILLUSTRATIONS

Cover Illustrations: Leland Klanderman

10–29: Judy Love. 36–37: Lindy Burnett. 38–59: Caroline Binch. 60–63: Robert McGuire. 65: Ken Bowser. 69: Sarah Beise. 80: Jason Abbott. 82–105: Pascal Biet. 116–139: Maya Christina Gonzalez. 146–147: Laura Ovresat. 160–183: Cat Bowman Smith. 240–241: Traci Van Wagoner. 248–269: DyAnne DiSalvo. 276: Kathleen Kemly. 279: Joe Taylor. 290–303: Helen Lester. 304–307: Susan Estelle Kwas. 314–339: Susan Kathleen Hartung. 362–385: Eileen Christelow. 386–389: Chris Boyd. 396–419: Javaka Steptoe. 424–425: Amanda Hall. 426–427: Cathi Mingus.

PHOTOGRAPHY

All Photographs are by Ken Cavanagh, Ken Karp or Dave Mager for Macmillan/McGraw Hill (MMH) except as noted below:

Inside front and back cover: Dynamic Graphics Group/Creatas/Alamy. v: Spencer Grant/Photo Edit. vi: William Dow/CORBIS. vii: (t) Superstock; (c) Darrell Wong/The Fresno Bee. ix: David Young-Wolff/Photo Edit. 2-3: BananaStock/PunchStock. 3: Michael Newman/PhotoEdit. 4: Michael Newman/PhotoEdit. 5: Maria Azucena Vigil. 6-7: Jeff Cadge/Getty Images. 8: (t) Don Tremain/Getty Images; (tr) Royalty Free/CORBIS. 9: David Young-Wolf/Photo Edit. 28: (tr) Courtesy Charlesbridge Press; (bl) Courtesy Charlesbridge Press. 30: Alan Oddie/Photo Edit. 31: Radius/PunchStock33: Amos Morgan/Photodisc/Punchstock. 34-35: Bill Bachmann/Index Stock Imagery. 58: (tl) Courtesy Mary Hoffman; (tr) Courtesy Caroline Binch. 66-67: Spencer Grant/Photo Edit. 68: (t) Jon Soo Hoo/Los Angeles Dodgers; (b) Major League Baseball/Urban Youth Academy. 69: Free the Children, www.freethechildren.com. 70-73: Bridget Barrett. 74: (tc) Bob Daemmrich/Photo Edit; (tr) Smart Creatives/Corbis. 78-79: Bettmann/CORBIS. 106-107: (bkgd) Tom Brakefield/The Image Works. 107: (tr) Robert E. Barber/Alamy; (c) Tom Brakefield/The Image Works, Inc. 108: (t) Johnansen Krause/National Geographic/Getty Images. 109: Jeff Lepore/Photo Researchers. 111: (r) © Image Source/Corbis. 112-113: CORBIS/PunchStock. 114: (tr) Tom Stewart/CORBIS; (bl) Michael Pole/CORBIS. 115: (cl) C Squared Studios/Getty Images. 138: (tr) Courtesy Children's Book Press; (cl) Courtesy Children's Book Press. 140: (l) Esselte/Phototone/Earthlink Textures; (bl) Marvin Koner/CORBIS. 141: (tl) Farrel Grehan/CORBIS; (bc) Western Pennsylvania Conservancy/Art Resource, NY. 142: (l) Esselte/Phototone/Earthlink Textures; (cr) Angelo Hornak/CORBIS; (c) Wetzel&Company. 143: Catherine Karnow/CORBIS. 145: Amos Morgan/Photodisc/Getty Images, Inc. 148: Nature Picture Library/Alamy. 149: Suzanne L. & Joseph T. Collins/Photo Researchers, Inc. 152-153: Jeff Greenberg/PhotoEdit. 153: Michael Newman/PhotoEdit. 154: Blend Images/Alamy. 155: Cathy Blaivis, Photographer. 156-157: The Art Archive/Culver Pictures. 158: (tr) Charles O'Rear/CORBIS; (cl) Michael Newman/Photo Edit; (bl) David Young-Wolff/Photo Edit. 159: Michael Newman/Photo Edit. 182: (tl) Courtesy Scholastic; (cl) Courtesy Cat Bowman Smith. 184: Bronwyn Kidd/Getty Images. 185: Lynda Richardson/CORBIS. 187: Ariel Skelley/CORBIS. 189: Amos Morgan/Photodisc/Punchstock. 190-191: Christi Carter/Grant Heilman Photography. 192: Millard H. Sharp/Photo Researchers. 193: (tr) Ken Thomas/Photo Researchers; (c) Valerie Giles/Photo Researchers. 194-195: William Dow/CORBIS. 196: (c) Ralph A. Clever/CORBIS; (bl) J.H. Pete Carmichael; (br) J.H. Pete Carmichael. 197: J.H. Pete Carmichael. 198-199: J.H. Pete Carmichael. 199: Whit Bronaugh. 200: (All Photos) Whit Bronaugh. 201: (tl) J.H. Pete Carmichael; (r) Whit Bronaugh. 202: Craig W. Racicot/Game Day Pictures. 203: Craig W. Racicot/Game Day Pictures. 204: (cl) J.H. Pete Carmichael; (cr) Ralph A. Clever/CORBIS; (br) J.H. Pete Carmichael. 204-205: Getty Images. 205: (tl) Craig W. Racicot/Game Day Pictures; (br) Whit Bronaugh. 206: Bill Beatty/Animals Animals/Earth Scenes. 206-207: Craig Tuttle/CORBIS. 207: (tr) Sharon Cummings/Dembinsky Photo Associates; (cl) Raymond Mendez/Animals Animals/Earth Scenes. 208: William Dow/CORBIS. 209: Frank Siteman/Photo Edit Inc. 210-211: Superstock. 212: Tom Bean/Corbis. 213: (tr) Tom Bean/Corbis; (cr) Glow Images/Alamy. 214: The Granger Collection, New York. 215-216: The Bancroft Library/University of California, Berkeley. 217: David Young-Wolff/Getty Images. 218: Yan Butchofsky/Corbis. 222-223: Creatas/PunchStock. 224: Peter Kaplan/Photo Researchers. 225: Heifer International. 226: Robert Cranston/RJ's Images of Nature. 227: Darrell Wong/The Fresno Bee.

Acknowledgments

228: Courtesy Stacey L. Caha. 229: Courtesy of The Fresno Bee. 230: Courtesy Stacey L. Caha. 231: Robert Cranston/RJ's Images of Nature. 232: David Hunter/The Fresno Bee. 233: Courtesy Stacey L. Caha. 234: Courtesy Stacey L. Caha. 235: Courtesy Stacey L. Caha. 236: Courtesy Stacey L. Caha. 237: Robert Cranston/RJ's Images of Nature. 238: Courtesy Gary Soto. 239: Robert Cranston/RJ's Images of Nature. 242: Darrell Wong/The Fresno Bee. 243: Amos Morgan/Photodisc/Getty Images, Inc. 244-245: Paul Burns/Photodisc/Getty Images. 246: Siede Preis/Getty Images. 246-247: Henry Diltz/CORBIS. 247: (tr) David Hiller/Photodisc blue/Getty Images; (c) Dennis MacDonald/Photo Edit. 268: Courtesy DyAnne DiSalvo. 270: (tr) Tim Matsui/Getty Images; (bl) Billy Hustace/Stone/Getty Images. 271: Erik S. Lesser/Getty Images. 272: Erik S. Lesser/Getty Images. 272-273: Mark Peterson/CORBIS. 275: Frank Siteman/PhotoEdit Inc. 278: (All Photos) Steve Ruark/Syracuse Newspapers/The Image Works. 279: Steve Ruark/Syracuse Newspapers/The Image Works. 282-283: IPNstock. 283: Ulana Switucha/Alamy. 284: ImageSource/PunchStock. 285: Courtesy Kathleen Krull. 286-287: Scott T. Smith/CORBIS. 288: Lulu Delacre. 289: (c) F. Schussler/Photolink/Getty Images; (cr) Siede Preis/Getty Images. 302: Courtesy Houghton Mifflin. 309: JupiterMedia/Alamy. 310-311: Craig Hammell/CORBIS. 312: (tr) Steve Cole/Masterfile; (cl) Paul Wenham-Clark/Masterfile; (bl) Jeff Greenberg/The Image Works. 313: (inset) Jeff Greenberg/The Image Works; (tr) Photodisc/Picture Quest. 338: (tl) Courtesy Soyung Pak; (cr)   Courtesy Susan Kathleen Hartung. 340: (bc) Underwood & Underwood/CORBIS; (br) Leonard de Selva/CORBIS. 341: (tr) J.

Richards/Alamy; (c) Leonard de Selva/CORBIS; (bl) Bettmann/CORBIS; (bc) National Archive/Newsmakers/Getty Images; (br) Roberts H. Armstrong/Robertstock/Retrofile. 342:(tr) Rubberball Productions/Getty Images; (cl) Photodisc/Getty Images; (b) Myrleen Ferguson Gate/Photo Edit. 343: (tr) Stewart Cohen/Stone/Getty Images. 345: Digital Vision/Punchstock. 346-347: David Young-Wolff/Photo Edit. 349: David Young-Wolff/Photo Edit. 354: Colin Young-Wolff/Photo Edit. 357: (c) Lars Lindblad/Shutterstock; (r) Siede Preis/Getty Images. 358-359: JIStock/Masterfile. 360: Bettman/CORBIS. 360-361: (top and bottom) C. Walker/Topham/The Image Works. 361: Bob Rowan/Progressive Image/CORBIS. 384: Courtesy Eileen Christelow. 388: (cr) CMCD/Getty Images; (br) ELIPSA/CORBIS Sygma. 389: (tr) Digital Vision/Getty Images; (cr) Robbie Jack/CORBIS. 391: Michael Newman/Photo Edit Inc. 392-393: LWA-Dann Tardif/CORBIS. 394: (tr) Royalty-Free/CORBIS; (bl) Royalty-Free/CORBIS. 395: (tl) The Image Bank/Getty Images; (cl) Royalty-Free/CORBIS; (cr) Bob Krist/CORBIS. 418: Courtesy Javaka Steptoe. 420: SuperStock. 421: Royalty-Free/CORBIS. 423: Pierre Arsenault/Masterfile. 430: (br) Jim Brandenburg/Minden Pictures; (bl) ©Royalty-Free/CORBIS. 432: © Kim Kulish/Corbis. 433: Stockbyte/PictureQuest. 434: Skip Nall/Getty Images, Inc. 435: Siede Preis/Getty Images, Inc. 436: © Randy Faris/Corbis. 437: Imagebroker/Alamy. 438: © APIX/Alamy. 439: PhotoLink/Getty Images, Inc. 440: ©Royalty-Free/CORBIS. 442: (t) © David Papazian/Corbis; (b) Digital Art/CORBIS. 444: Margot Granitsas/The Image Works, Inc. 445: C Squared Studios/Getty Images, Inc. IBC: Dynamic Graphics Group/Creatas/Alamy.

Reading/Language Arts
CA California Standards
Grade 3

READING

1.0 Word Analysis, Fluency, and Systematic Vocabulary Development

Students understand the basic features of reading. They select letter patterns and know how to translate them into spoken language by using phonics, syllabication, and word parts. They apply this knowledge to achieve fluent oral and silent reading.

Decoding and Word Recognition

1.1	Know and use complex word families when reading (e.g., *-ight*) to decode unfamiliar words.
1.2	Decode regular multisyllabic words.
1.3	Read aloud narrative and expository text fluently and accurately and with appropriate pacing, intonation, and expression.

Vocabulary and Concept Development

1.4	Use knowledge of antonyms, synonyms, homophones, and homographs to determine the meanings of words.
1.5	Demonstrate knowledge of levels of specificity among grade-appropriate words and explain the importance of these relations (e.g., *dog/ mammal/ animal/ living things*).
1.6	Use sentence and word context to find the meaning of unknown words.
1.7	Use a dictionary to learn the meaning and other features of unknown words.
1.8	Use knowledge of prefixes (e.g., *un-, re-, pre-, bi-, mis-, dis-*) and suffixes (e.g., *-er, -est, -ful*) to determine the meaning of words.

2.0 Reading Comprehension

Students read and understand grade-level-appropriate material. They draw upon a variety of comprehension strategies as needed (e.g., generating and responding to essential questions, making predictions, comparing information from several sources). The selections in *Recommended Literature, Kindergarten Through Grade Twelve* illustrate the quality and complexity of the materials to be read by students. In addition to their regular school reading, by grade four, students read one-half million words annually, including a good representation of grade-level-appropriate narrative and expository text (e.g., classic and contemporary literature, magazines, newspapers, online information). In grade three, students make substantial progress toward this goal.

READING (continued)

Structural Features of Informational Materials

2.1 Use titles, tables of contents, chapter headings, glossaries, and indexes to locate information in text.

Comprehension and Analysis of Grade-Level-Appropriate Text

2.2 Ask questions and support answers by connecting prior knowledge with literal information found in, and inferred from, the text.

2.3 Demonstrate comprehension by identifying answers in the text.

2.4 Recall major points in the text and make and modify predictions about forthcoming information.

2.5 Distinguish the main idea and supporting details in expository text.

2.6 Extract appropriate and significant information from the text, including problems and solutions.

2.7 Follow simple multiple-step written instructions (e.g., how to assemble a product or play a board game).

3.0 Literary Response and Analysis Students read and respond to a wide variety of significant works of children's literature. They distinguish between the structural features of the text and literary terms or elements (e.g., theme, plot, setting, characters). The selections in *Recommended Literature, Kindergarten Through Grade Twelve* illustrate the quality and complexity of the materials to be read by students.

Structural Features of Literature

3.1 Distinguish common forms of literature (e.g., poetry, drama, fiction, nonfiction).

Narrative Analysis of Grade-Level-Appropriate Text

3.2 Comprehend basic plots of classic fairy tales, myths, folktales, legends, and fables from around the world.

3.3 Determine what characters are like by what they say or do and by how the author or illustrator portrays them.

3.4 Determine the underlying theme or author's message in fiction and nonfiction text.

3.5 Recognize the similarities of sounds in words and rhythmic patterns (e.g., alliteration, onomatopoeia) in a selection.

3.6 Identify the speaker or narrator in a selection.

WRITING

1.0 Writing Strategies Students write clear and coherent sentences and paragraphs that develop a central idea. Their writing shows they consider the audience and purpose. Students progress through the stages of the writing process (e.g., prewriting, drafting, revising, editing successive versions).

Organization and Focus

1.1 Create a single paragraph:
    a. Develop a topic sentence.
    b. Include simple supporting facts and details.

Penmanship

1.2 Write legibly in cursive or joined italic, allowing margins and correct spacing between letters in a word and words in a sentence.

Research

1.3 Understand the structure and organization of various reference materials (e.g., dictionary, thesaurus, atlas, encyclopedia).

Evaluation and Revision

1.4 Revise drafts to improve the coherence and logical progression of ideas by using an established rubric.

2.0 Writing Applications (Genres and Their Characteristics) Students write compositions that describe and explain familiar objects, events, and experiences. Student writing demonstrates a command of standard American English and the drafting, research, and organizational strategies outlined in Writing Standard 1.0.

Using the writing strategies of grade three outlined in Writing Standard 1.0, students:

2.1 Write narratives:
    a. Provide a context within which an action takes place.
    b. Include well-chosen details to develop the plot.
    c. Provide insight into why the selected incident is memorable.

2.2 Write descriptions that use concrete sensory details to present and support unified impressions of people, places, things, or experiences.

2.3 Write personal and formal letters, thank-you notes, and invitations:
    a. Show awareness of the knowledge and interests of the audience and establish a purpose and context.
    b. Include the date, proper salutation, body, closing, and signature.

WRITTEN AND ORAL ENGLISH LANGUAGE CONVENTIONS

The standards for written and oral English language conventions have been placed between those for writing and for listening and speaking because these conventions are essential to both sets of skills.

1.0 Written and Oral English Language Conventions Students write and speak with a command of standard English conventions appropriate to this grade level.

Sentence Structure

1.1 Understand and be able to use complete and correct declarative, interrogative, imperative, and exclamatory sentences in writing and speaking.

Grammar

1.2 Identify subjects and verbs that are in agreement and identify and use pronouns, adjectives, compound words, and articles correctly in writing and speaking.

1.3 Identify and use past, present, and future verb tenses properly in writing and speaking.

1.4 Identify and use subjects and verbs correctly in speaking and writing simple sentences.

Punctuation

1.5 Punctuate dates, city and state, and titles of books correctly.

1.6 Use commas in dates, locations, and addresses and for items in a series.

Capitalization

1.7 Capitalize geographical names, holidays, historical periods, and special events correctly.

Spelling

1.8 Spell correctly one-syllable words that have blends, contractions, compounds, orthographic patterns (e.g., *qu*, consonant doubling, changing the ending of a word from -y to -ies when forming the plural), and common homophones (e.g., *hair-hare*).

1.9 Arrange words in alphabetic order.

LISTENING AND SPEAKING

1.0 Listening and Speaking Strategies Students listen critically and respond appropriately to oral communication. They speak in a manner that guides the listener to understand important ideas by using proper phrasing, pitch, and modulation.

Comprehension

1.1   Retell, paraphrase, and explain what has been said by a speaker.

1.2   Connect and relate prior experiences, insights, and ideas to those of a speaker.

1.3   Respond to questions with appropriate elaboration.

1.4   Identify the musical elements of literary language (e.g., rhymes, repeated sounds, instances of onomatopoeia).

Organization and Delivery of Oral Communication

1.5   Organize ideas chronologically or around major points of information.

1.6   Provide a beginning, a middle, and an end, including concrete details that develop a central idea.

1.7   Use clear and specific vocabulary to communicate ideas and establish the tone.

1.8   Clarify and enhance oral presentations through the use of appropriate props (e.g., objects, pictures, charts).

1.9   Read prose and poetry aloud with fluency, rhythm, and pace, using appropriate intonation and vocal patterns to emphasize important passages of the text being read.

Analysis and Evaluation of Oral and Media Communications

1.10   Compare ideas and points of view expressed in broadcast and print media.

1.11   Distinguish between the speaker's opinions and verifiable facts.

2.0 Speaking Applications (Genres and Their Characteristics) Students deliver brief recitations and oral presentations about familiar experiences or interests that are organized around a coherent thesis statement. Student speaking demonstrates a command of standard American English and the organizational and delivery strategies outlined in Listening and Speaking Standard 1.0.

Using the speaking strategies of grade three outlined in Listening and Speaking Standard 1.0, students:

2.1   Make brief narrative presentations:
     a. Provide a context for an incident that is the subject of the presentation.
     b. Provide insight into why the selected incident is memorable.
     c. Include well-chosen details to develop character, setting, and plot.

2.2   Plan and present dramatic interpretations of experiences, stories, poems, or plays with clear diction, pitch, tempo, and tone.

2.3   Make descriptive presentations that use concrete sensory details to set forth and support unified impressions of people, places, things, or experiences.